# Integrating CRM Across Your Organization for Business Success

---

Build your business processes around the needs of your
customers by successfully integrating your CRM within your
core business functions to drive improvement

---

## Andrew Blackmore

Impackt Publishing
We Mean Business

# Integrating CRM Across Your Organization for Business Success

First published: January 2016

Production reference: 1180116

Published by Impackt Publishing Ltd.
Livery Place
35 Livery Street
Birmingham B3 2PB, UK.

ISBN 978-1-78300-104-0

www.Impacktpub.com

# Credits

**Author**
Andrew Blackmore

**Reviewer**
Davy Pelssers

**Acquisition Editor**
Richard Gall

**Content Development Editor**
Vaibhav Pawar

**Copy Editor**
Tanvi Bhatt

**Project Coordinator**
Priyanka Goel

**Proofreaders**
Simran Bhogal
Maria Gould
Paul Hindle

**Graphics**
Jason Monteiro

**Production Coordinator**
Melwyn D'sa

**Cover Work**
Melwyn D'sa

# About the Author

 **Andrew Blackmore** works for Sage Software Solutions in Vancouver. He has spent the last 15 years leading the development of integrations between CRM and ERP applications all over the world, using every different technology available and for any conceivable business use case. Over that time, he has built up a large store of experience and knowledge that he is imparting in this book. He has seen first-hand the business benefit of integrating CRM in organizations and has a deep familiarity of the techniques and solutions in this book.

Andrew's passion is developing software in an ingenious way to build efficient, innovative solutions that provide a real lasting business benefit for customers. He is currently working on the new cloud and mobile solutions projects for Sage.

I would like to thank my wife and family for their support and encouragement.

# About the Reviewer

**Davy Pelssers** is a freelance SAP CRM and SAP CRM Authorizations consultant. He started his SAP consulting career in 2000, and since then has worked within several SAP modules in the past such as SAP IS-U, SAP BW, SAP CRM, and SAP Authorizations. For the past 10 years, his focus has been in the area of SAP Customer Relationship Management and SAP CRM Authorizations. In this last area, he has become a real expert due to his profound research. His main strengths are his capability to creatively design solutions for complex customer requirements, his persistence in solving issues, and his drive to always learn new things.

Davy is founder of the company Dasap Consulting BVBA and is located in Belgium.

He is also the owner of the website www.sapuniversity.eu where a group of motivated SAP consultants from over the world share their knowledge by writing useful articles about the established SAP modules.

# Contents

| | |
|---|---|
| **Preface** | **1** |
| **Chapter 1: What is CRM Integration and Why is It Good for Your Business?** | **5** |
| Different CRM applications | 5 |
| Workshop | 7 |
| Users, user roles, and teams | 7 |
| Workshop | 8 |
| How workflows are used in CRM | 8 |
| Security in CRM | 9 |
| Contact management | 9 |
| Contact management workflows | 10 |
| Integration opportunity for contact management | 11 |
| Workshop | 12 |
| Sales management | 12 |
| Sales management workflow | 13 |
| Integration opportunity for sales management | 14 |
| Workshop | 14 |
| Customer support | 15 |
| Customer support workflow | 15 |
| Integration opportunity for customer support | 16 |
| Workshop | 17 |
| Management information | 17 |
| Integration opportunity for management information | 18 |
| Workshop | 19 |
| Summary | 19 |
| **Chapter 2: How to Implement an Integration** | **21** |
| Build or buy | 21 |
| Workshop | 22 |
| Building an integration | 22 |
| Challenge 1 – extract the data | 24 |
| Direct access from database | 24 |

| | |
|---|---|
| Access through business (API) | 25 |
| Screen popping | 26 |
| Workshop | 26 |
| Challenge 2 – transporting the data between ERP and CRM | 26 |
| Synchronized data | 27 |
| Synchronization architecture options | 29 |
| Real time data views | 34 |
| Workshop | 36 |
| Challenge 3 – storing the data in CRM | 36 |
| How to store the data in CRM | 37 |
| Workshop | 39 |
| Challenge 4 – displaying the data in CRM UI | 39 |
| Adding fields to screens or lists | 40 |
| Adding new screens or lists | 40 |
| Adding new buttons to launch other features | 41 |
| Adding CRM reports or dashboards | 45 |
| Workshop | 46 |
| Summary | 47 |

## Chapter 3: How to Build a Contact Integration      49

| | |
|---|---|
| Contact management integration scenario | 49 |
| Integration workflows | 50 |
| Promoting CRM customers to ERP | 51 |
| Automatic synchronization of ERP customers from ERP to CRM | 52 |
| Viewing ERP customer information on CRM customer screens | 52 |
| Designing the integration | 52 |
| Step 1 – entity diagrams | 53 |
| Entity diagram for SageCRM customers | 53 |
| Entity diagram for Sage ERP 300 customers | 54 |
| Workshop | 55 |
| Step 2 – mapping the entity diagrams to each other | 55 |
| Entity mapping | 55 |
| Customers | 56 |
| Contacts | 56 |
| Address | 57 |
| Phone number | 57 |
| E-mail address | 57 |
| Summary of entity mapping | 58 |
| Workshop | 58 |
| Step 3 – defining the unique identifiers | 59 |
| Strategies for uniquely identifying records | 59 |
| Using a unique identifier such as database IDs or reference numbers | 60 |
| Use a parent/child relationship of the entities | 61 |
| Summary of unique identifiers | 63 |
| Workshop | 63 |
| Step 4 – defining the fields and field mappings | 64 |
| Customer field mapping | 64 |
| Contact field mappings | 68 |
| Address field mappings | 69 |

| | |
|---|---|
| Phone number field mappings | 70 |
| E-mail field mappings | 70 |
| Workshop | 71 |
| Step 5 – defining the CRUD rules | 71 |
| Synchronizing create actions on ERP and CRM | 71 |
| Importing ERP customers to CRM in bulk | 72 |
| Newly created ERP customers should be synchronized to CRM | 72 |
| Qualified CRM customers should be "promoted" to ERP | 72 |
| Limiting other creation use cases | 74 |
| Summary of synch creation use cases | 75 |
| Synchronizing update actions on CRM and ERP | 76 |
| Summary of synch update use cases | 77 |
| Synchronizing delete actions on CRM and ERP | 77 |
| Summary of synch delete use cases | 78 |
| Workshop | 79 |
| Security | 79 |
| Security for "read" information | 79 |
| Security for create, update, and delete information | 80 |
| Security summary | 80 |
| Workshop | 80 |
| CRM UI changes | 81 |
| UI changes to customer screens | 81 |
| UI changes to contact screens | 82 |
| UI changes to address screens | 82 |
| UI changes to e-mail address screens | 82 |
| Administration screen | 82 |
| Reports/dashboard changes | 83 |
| Workshop | 83 |
| Summary | 83 |
| **Chapter 4: How to Build a Sales Management Integration** | **85** |
| Sales management integration use cases | 85 |
| Integration workflows | 86 |
| Ability to create quotes and orders | 87 |
| How | 87 |
| Ability to view quote and order history | 87 |
| How | 87 |
| Design the integration | 87 |
| Step 1 – creating entity diagrams | 88 |
| Step 2 – mapping the entity diagrams to each other | 89 |
| Step 3 – defining the unique identifiers | 89 |
| Workshop | 91 |
| Step 4 – defining the fields and field mappings | 91 |
| Workshop | 95 |
| Step 5 – defining the CRUD rules | 95 |
| Creating quotes, orders, and line items | 96 |
| Updating quotes or orders | 97 |
| Deleting quotes or orders | 97 |

Summary of CUD actions     97
    Workshop     98
Step 6 – designing the screen pops     98
    Authentication for the ERP screen     99
    Customer unique reference     99
    Quote or order unique reference     99
    Linking a quote or order with a CRM user     99
    Location of the buttons     100
    Workshop     100
Security     100
    Orders and quotes that are viewable in CRM     101
    Creating and editing orders and quotes     101
    Security summary     102
    Workshop     102
CRM UI changes     102
    New screens that need to be built     104
    Report/dashboard changes     105
    Workshop     105
Advanced workshop discussion     105
Summary     107

**Chapter 5: How to Build a Collections Management Integration**     **109**

Collections management integration use cases     109
Integration workflows     110
    Ability to view ERP invoices in CRM     111
    How     111
Security     119
CRM UI changes     120
    New screens that need to be built     122
Reports/dashboard changes     123
Advanced workshop checklist     123
Summary     126

**Chapter 6: How to Build a Vendor Management Integration**     **127**

Vendor management integration use cases     127
Integration workflows     128
    Ability to view ERP vendors in CRM     129
    How?     129
Security     137
CRM UI changes     138
    Changes to CRM company screens     138
    UI changes to child entity screens     138
    Vendor integration with the CRM interactions feature     139
Reports/dashboard changes     139
Advanced workshop checklist     140
Summary     143

## Chapter 7: How to Build a Support Management Integration     145

| | |
|---|---|
| Support management integration use cases | 145 |
|   Integration workflows | 146 |
|    How | 146 |
| Security | 149 |
| CRM UI changes | 149 |
| Advanced workshop checklist | 149 |
| Summary | 150 |

## Chapter 8: How to Develop and Maintain Your Integration     153

| | |
|---|---|
| Development plan | 153 |
|   Work areas | 154 |
|   User stories | 155 |
|    Schema work area story examples | 155 |
|    Server work are story examples | 156 |
|    UI work area story examples | 156 |
|    Installation work area story examples | 157 |
|   Estimates | 157 |
|   Implementing the user stories | 158 |
| Deployment | 158 |
|   Installing the new integration feature | 159 |
|   Bringing users live | 159 |
| Ongoing maintenance | 160 |
|   Fixing defects | 160 |
|   Periodic upgrades of ERP and CRM | 161 |
|   Data management – backups and manual synchronization | 161 |
|   Adding new integration features | 161 |
| Summary | 162 |

## Chapter 9: Where Next for Integrations – the Cloud and Other Areas     163

| | |
|---|---|
| The future of RideRight Bike Parts Company | 163 |
| Moving CRM and ERP to the cloud | 164 |
| Making mobile apps available to CRM users | 164 |
| Customers running things themselves | 165 |
| Summary of the chapter | 166 |
| Conclusion | 166 |

# > Preface

Every business that deals with customers has a CRM application of some kind to manage customer interactions, and an accounting or ERP application of some kind to deal with financial transactions. Even though the business process of managing customers is directly related to the business goal of making new financial transactions, these two applications are rarely integrated.

This book is dedicated to showing you how to build an integration between your CRM and ERP applications.

I have spent most of my career working on systems integration projects. I have spent the last thirteen years with Sage Plc, a global business management software company, building integrations between CRM and ERP applications. Sage produces over twenty ERP applications–from tier 1 single-user accounting applications to tier 5 enterprise-level ERPs–in different geographies across Europe, North America, Asia, Australia, and Africa, and it has integrated most of them with its CRM application, Sage CRM, and other CRM applications. This has given me a very wide range of integration experiences with many different technology stacks and features.

This book is aimed at anyone who is thinking about building an integration between any CRM and ERP application. You could be an IT manager, project manager, or developer in a business that uses any decent CRM and ERP application, or a business partner or development partner for any commercial CRM or ERP application. You could be thinking about building an integration from scratch, or extending an existing integration.

The structure of the book is designed to take you, in a logical sequence, through all stages of building an integration; from a discussion of the business benefits of building an integration, through how to build an integration, which features to build, and how to project manage the implementation. I have kept the scope of the projects at the low end of the scale, always avoiding super complex architectures and designs so that they can be implemented by one or two good developers.

At the end of the chapters, there are advanced workshop checklists, which are aimed at exploring alternatives, shortcuts, improvements, and different design approaches that you can take. You should follow through the design of a feature, and once there is an understanding of the design goals, you should go through the advanced workshop section to evaluate alternatives that may be more suitable for your own particular situation.

Once you have read through the chapters and completed the workshops and advanced workshop sections, you should have all you need to start your integration project. You should have a business justification for implementing your integration, an integration architecture for your integration, and detailed designs for each of your integration features, all tailored to your CRM and ERP applications. You should have a resource plan and project plan for implementation and deployment, and an ongoing plan for support and maintenance of the integration.

# What this book covers

The book takes you through all stages of building an integration, including a discussion of the business benefits of integrations, how to architect and design an integration, which features you should build that are of most benefit to you and your business, and how you will project manage and develop the integration.

*Chapter 1, What is CRM Integration and Why is It Good For Your Business*, talks about what we mean by an integration that links a CRM application with an ERP application, what are the business processes that will be affected by an integration, and most importantly, why we do it—what are the business benefits that you will achieve. The chapter also introduces some of the terminology that will be used throughout the book.

*Chapter 2, How to Implement an Integration*, is technology focused, where we look at some of the different integration architectures that are available and the building blocks and components that are needed for building an integration. Many technical concepts that will be used throughout the book are introduced in this chapter.

In the subsequent five chapters, we design for specific integration scenarios. The first scenario is common to all the integration solutions, and then you can look at the other integration features and check out which ones are interesting for you right now, and which ones may be put off to a later phase.

In each chapter, we take you very carefully through all the design steps, using examples along the way. We cover all areas that are affected by the integration; backend changes, schema changes, user interface changes, security, and reporting. Within each chapter, there are workshops containing questions, evaluations, and research topics. The intention of the workshops is to prompt you to do your own parallel planning and design as you move through the book. Each workshop section contains important decision points that need to be resolved by anyone who is doing an integration.

*Chapter 3, How to Build a Contact Integration*, is where we design an integration for contact management, allowing your CRM users to improve how they manage their customer relationships. The contact management integration is a fundamental feature of any CRM to ERP integration, linking customers and contact information such as phone numbers and addresses between CRM and ERP, thereby removing the need for double entry of data and keeping your information consistent across the business. As this is the first chapter to talk about integration design, we take you very carefully through all the design steps, using detailed examples to explain each step of the process.

*Chapter 4, How to Build a Sales Management Integration*, is where we design an integration for sales management, for the benefit of your sales team and sales managers. Sales management integration brings in efficiencies and improvements in your sales team's productivity by linking the sales quotes and sales orders in ERP with the contact management and sales opportunity functionality in CRM.

*Chapter 5, How to Build a Collections Management Integration*, is where we design an integration for collections management to improve your business's cash flow. Collections management integration speeds up the collection of unpaid invoices from your delinquent accounts by linking sales invoices in ERP with your powerful CRM contact management functionality.

*Chapter 6, How to Build a Vendor Management Integration*, is where we design an integration to manage your vendor relationships for the benefit of your purchasing team and any other members of your business who deal with vendors. The vendor management integration provides a simple vendor management tool by linking your ERP vendor lists to' your powerful CRM contact management functionality.

*Chapter 7, How to Build a Support Management Integration*, is where we design a support management integration for the benefit of your customer support team and any team members who deal with customer issues and complaints. The support management integration can make your support team's workflow more seamless, transparent, and efficient by linking CRM support features with ERP functionality.

*Chapter 8, How to Develop and Maintain Your Integration*, after you have designed your integration, it needs to be implemented. We provide you with some simple project management techniques and examples that can be used during the building, deployment, and ongoing support and maintenance of the integration.

*Chapter 9, Where Next for Integrations–the Cloud and Other Areas*, discusses how technology changes will affect the future of integrations between CRM and ERP.

# Who this book is for

This section needs to be added by the Technical Editor after discussing with the Development Editor.

# Conventions

In this book, you will find a number of styles of text that distinguish between different kinds of information. Here are some examples of these styles, and an explanation of their meaning.

**New terms** and **important words** are shown in bold.

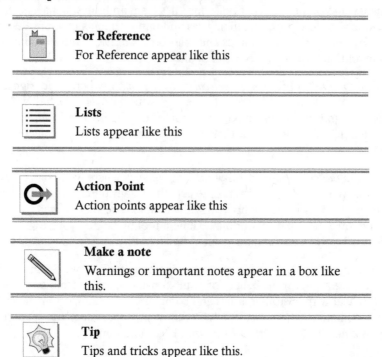

| | **For Reference** |
|---|---|
| | For Reference appear like this |

| | **Lists** |
|---|---|
| | Lists appear like this |

| | **Action Point** |
|---|---|
| | Action points appear like this |

| | **Make a note** |
|---|---|
| | Warnings or important notes appear in a box like this. |

| | **Tip** |
|---|---|
| | Tips and tricks appear like this. |

# Reader feedback

Feedback from our readers is always welcome. Let us know what you think about this book—what you liked or may have disliked. Reader feedback is important for us to develop titles that you really get the most out of.

To send us general feedback, simply send an e-mail to feedback@impacktpub.com, and mention the book title via the subject of your message.

If there is a book that you need and would like to see us publish, please send us a note via the **Submit Idea** form on https://www.impacktpub.com/#!/bookidea.

# Piracy

Piracy of copyright material on the Internet is an ongoing problem across all media. At Packt, we take the protection of our copyright and licenses very seriously. If you come across any illegal copies of our works, in any form, on the Internet, please provide us with the location address or website name immediately so that we can pursue a remedy.

Please contact us at copyright@impacktpub.com with a link to the suspected pirated material.

We appreciate your help in protecting our authors, and our ability to bring you valuable content.

# >1

# What is CRM Integration and Why is It Good for Your Business?

This book is about how to build a CRM integration with your ERP. In this chapter, we talk about what we mean by CRM integration and the different ways that it can be good for your business.

To get started, we briefly discuss some terminology and concepts that will be used throughout the book: users, user roles and teams, and security in a CRM application, and why they are affected by integration. We will then explore the benefits of different business workflows in CRM and how they become more powerful when they become integrated business workflow. We will also talk about specific areas of CRM functionality and how they benefit from being integrated with ERP.

Finally, at the end of this chapter we will explore how what we have discussed can be applied to your business.

## Different CRM applications

Even though every business manages their customer relationships, not every business has a CRM application.

If you are self-employed running your own business with little or no staff, you may use very basic free contact management functionality on your mobile phone or you may use a simple spreadsheet, or e-mail, to manage your customers.

If your business is more than just one person, the next step up could be a basic contact management tool such as Goldmine or ACT!

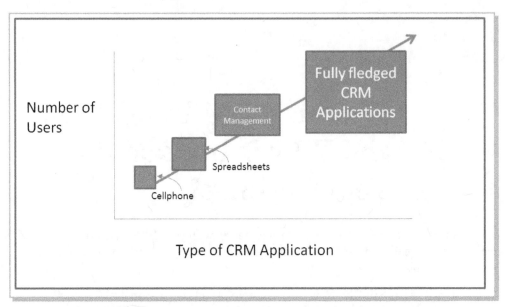

*As the number of users increases the complexity of your CRM solution tends to increase*

Real CRM, however, comes in a level higher than simple contact management tools. It is more suitable for businesses big enough to have several people, or teams, performing different functions. In this case a more fully featured CRM application is justified.

One class of CRM application is online systems such as **SugarCRM** or **Zoho CRM**. Fuller CRM functionality is available in CRM applications such as **SalesLogix**, **SalesForce**, or **Microsoft Dynamics CRM**. My background is with the **SageCRM** application by Sage, which is also a fully featured CRM application available both online and on premises.

For this book, we are not going to focus on any specific CRM application, but we are talking about CRM applications with well-developed features such as contact or customer management, sales, customer support, and marketing modules. There may be optional add on extensions such as customer self-service, or support for mobile.

We will talk about modifying the CRM application to integrate it with ERP. The CRM application will therefore need to have some way of being customized and extended. It will preferably have a development API or toolkits, of some kind. These are to be expected with any decent CRM application.

Have a look at your high-level CRM checklist:

| | |
|---|---|
| **Fully featured** <br> ■ Contact management <br> ■ Sales management <br> ■ Support management <br> ■ Marketing | |
| **Customizable** <br> ■ Tools or development API available <br> ■ Ability to customize screens, and extend your CRM application | |

As we go through the benefits of integration, it is never too early be thinking of how you will develop the customizations and integration. Do you have in-house skills to implement customization and integrations, or will you have to outsource the work? We will talk more about that in the next chapter.

# Workshop

Now take some time to consider the following questions:

> ➤ Is the CRM application that you use suitable for integration? Consider the features that it has and how easy is it to customize; is there a development API?

> ➤ Does your business have the development skills to develop an integration? These skills could be in-house, or contractors, or business partners. Have you or has anyone in your organization run a development project before? Are you comfortable to take one on?

The rest of this chapter is a discussion of the common CRM concepts and features that we will need as a basis for building our CRM integration, and how they are affected by CRM integration.

# Users, user roles, and teams

We use the term *users* to refer to people who use a CRM or an ERP application.

Typical users of a CRM application are people in your organization who are customer-facing; they have to interact with customers as part of their daily duties. We will focus on the more common areas where people work with customers, such as sales, customer support, and marketing.

The users of the ERP application are typically more back-office focused. Accountants and bookkeepers will use an ERP application rather than a CRM application.

We use the term *roles* to refer to the work that our users do.

In small businesses users may perform more than one role. Salespeople may also do a marketing function one day a week for example. In larger organizations the function will be made up of *teams* of users; for example one or more sales teams, a support team, and a marketing team.

If the business is more complex there could be some granularity to these roles. In sales, for example, there may be an inside sales role for those who do sales from within the office, and/or an outside sales role for salespeople who travel outside the office.

When you are designing your integration you will need to think about users, user roles, and teams. Can your users be grouped under common roles such as sales role or support role? Do you have multiple teams performing the same role, for example do you have different sales teams, perhaps separated geographically, or by business unit? As we talk later about different integration features, you will need to think about how they apply to your business, and which users, roles, and teams in your business are going to benefit the most.

# Workshop

Consider the following questions to help get a stronger understanding of who is likely to be involved and how with your CRM integration:

- ➤ Do you know who uses your CRM application?
- ➤ Have you identified teams and other people who use your application? Is there a distinction between sales, support, and marketing users?
- ➤ Do you have any other roles in your business?
- ➤ Do you have multiple teams performing the same role?
- ➤ Who are the managers and team leaders?

# How workflows are used in CRM

Every user has work to do, and in a well-run business they are they usually following a specific process. In CRM, the features that support a business process are called a **workflow**, or **business workflow**. A workflow is the set of actions that is undertaken to perform a multi-step procedure or task.

Usually, the set of actions will take place over a period of time; days, or maybe even weeks. The set of actions will need to be done in sequence. It can involve multiple users, or teams, and it can involve work by users in different roles.

A sales workflow is a classic example. A sales workflow could be the process of taking a lead, and qualifying it, perhaps going through several stages, involving meetings with your customer, phone calls, quotations, and so on, to get to the point where a sale is made.

Workflows are interesting in CRM because in many cases they are unique to your business, and workflows in CRM therefore need to be modifiable for your business. Most CRM applications allow you to customize your workflow to suit your own business process.

For example, while every business has a sales workflow, each business will do it differently depending on what they are selling, and what their business model is. Some businesses may do aggressive cold calling for new customers, while others may wait for new clients to come to them, and yet others may mainly deal with existing customers. For a CRM application to be useful, it has to be flexible enough to fit in with most business models. CRM applications do this by having flexible, customizable workflows.

This is useful for us when we are developing an integration. The development of an integration will necessarily mean that workflows will be changed from the way they were with a non-integrated CRM. We will be able to do this because CRM workflows are flexible and customizable.

It can be argued that this is precisely the point of integrating your CRM with an ERP. Having a separate CRM and ERP application means you have separate workflows, which can result in a disconnection—not a good recipe for a quality customer experience. Having a CRM to ERP integration allows you to unify your workflows and bring efficiencies, and connectedness and a better customer experience.

# Security in CRM

Security is important. Security is focused on the data, and in particular what data your users are allowed to see. You do not want members of your sales team exporting or printing off the entire customer list and selling it to a competitor.

When you implement an integration with ERP, security needs to be considered carefully in the design. Financial information in an ERP can be even more sensitive than CRM information, and some ERP financial data, such as credit limit, or total sales amounts, may become available to your sales or support team for the first time.

The challenge for an integration is that the security model in the CRM application is unlikely to be the same as the one in the ERP application. The next chapter discusses some approaches to security management for your integrated data.

# Contact management

We are going to discuss several features in CRM applications that are useful to be integrated with ERP. The first one is **contact management**.

Contact management gives users the ability to view, manage, and communicate with their customers. Contact management is the foundational feature for any CRM solution. Contacts include the names of the customers or businesses that you are working with, and the names of the contacts or people who work for the businesses.

With a non-integrated CRM application, if you are doing business with the customer the same customer information will need to be entered again in the ERP application, resulting in the same data being entered twice and a disconnected process.

# Contact management workflows

In CRM, the creation of a customer can be straightforward, for example by simply adding a customer's name, and a contact name to the CRM application. To make it useful, you would need some more information such as a phone number or an e-mail address.

A more sophisticated workflow is the creation of a customer from a lead. A business can gather a list of leads, from say, a website, a tradeshow, or by purchasing a data from a third party. You will then need to qualify the leads by converting the raw data to a good quality list of potential customers.

The workflow to qualify leads into customers who you are going to potentially sell to, is an example of a more complex contact management workflow:

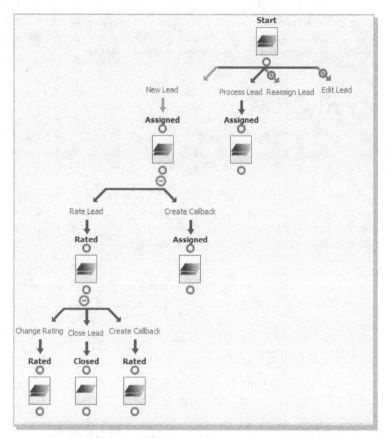

*Example of a lead qualification workflow state diagram in SageCRM*

A lead qualification workflow may have some or all of the following steps:

> **Check data**: This could be a manual inspection of the lead to ensure that there is enough information to make contact with the customer—for example, is there a first name and a last name, a phone number, an address, or an e-mail address?

➤ **Verify data**: The address, zip code, and other contact information for the lead might be verified by using a third-party address verification system, for example.

➤ **Make contact with the lead**: This could be an attempted cold phone call, mailer, or sending an e-mail out to the lead to determine interest.

➤ **Contact achieved**: If a contact is achieved with the lead, the lead could be converted to a qualified lead, or a potential customer. This would typically move the lead on to a further step in the workflow, or into a sales workflow, where a sales user would attempt to make a sale. Refer to the next section to see the sales workflow.

In an ERP we also store customer information because the ERP is used to send sales quotes, orders, invoices, and shipments to customers. While the ERP is not involved in lead qualification, there is a workflow around the creation of customers, which in ERP are called accounts receivable customers, or A/R customers.

If the ERP is not integrated with CRM, similar customer information that you have added to CRM will also have to be added to ERP. It is interesting to note that the customer information that will to be added to the ERP tends to be a higher quality and is more financially-oriented.

This is because the information that is added to ERP will be used to send valuable documents such as invoices and for the shipping of goods, which are worth money. In order to ensure that the customer is able to pay, and is charged the correct amount, financially important information needs to be captured such as tax information, payment terms, and credit limits.

In an integration between CRM and ERP, it is possible to take advantage of the fact that similar customer information is used in both CRM and ERP.

# Integration opportunity for contact management

A non-integrated CRM application is not optimal for doing contact management because it means you need to maintain two separate customer lists, one in CRM and the other in ERP, both of which contain very similar information.

Your ERP contains the full list of the existing customers who you are selling to. Integrating this information with your CRM gives you the contacts you should be communicating with from your CRM system for your existing customers.

If you pull the data from ERP to CRM, you will avoid entering data twice, and connect some of your business processes. The contact information that comes from ERP will be of higher quality and so it will be more useful to your sales users. The customers' data in ERP will also have useful information such as whether or not they are on credit hold, or what their credit limit and payment terms are. This could be useful to a sales person taking an order within the CRM application.

On the CRM side, your new customers and prospects are likely to start off as leads or customers in the CRM system. Integrating with the ERP allows you to automatically promote customers to ERP when you are going to start providing them with quotes, taking orders, and generally doing financial business with them, preventing data from being entered twice.

# Workshop

Briefly outline the process by which leads and contacts are harvested for your CRM application and how A/R customers are entered for your ERP application. Can you see a benefit in linking these two workflows so that CRM customers are "promoted" to ERP, and/or A/R customers in ERP are copied to CRM?

# Sales management

The sales management feature is usually the most popular feature in a CRM application. Sales management is for helping your sales team make sales to new and existing customers.

We call the feature that is used to keep track of each sales opportunity in the CRM application an *opportunity* or *sales opportunity*. In non-integrated CRM, once a sale is made and an order is taken, the sales user will need to use the ERP application to process the order, resulting data being entered twice, and a disconnected process.

A sales pipeline is a snapshot view of how your sales opportunities are progressing. Some opportunities may be newly created, some may be in progress, and some may have been completed, either by a sale coming through, or they may have failed. The sales pipeline will give you a view of this:

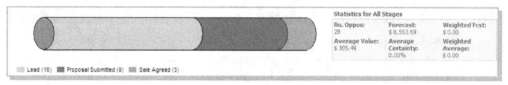

*SageCRM Sales Pipeline*

In non-integrated CRM, the sales pipeline only shows how you are progressing with a sale until the order is placed in the ERP, because the CRM will not know what happens after the business process moves to the ERP.

Sales opportunities have items in them for sales, and in CRM we call them **products**. Products may be services, or they may be physical things, with an inventory associated with them. For example, a company that sells services may not have an inventory, but a company that sells physical items will be likely to have an inventory of their items.

This is a key integration point, because the inventory is stored in ERP, and is not usually available in a non-integrated CRM application. Getting the inventory into CRM is a useful integration feature.

# Sales management workflow

We call the process used to manage the business process for how sales opportunities are tracked in your company the sales workflow. As sales is such an important part of any business there may be several different sales workflows depending on what is being sold. The following diagram shows a part of a sales workflow state diagram from SageCRM:

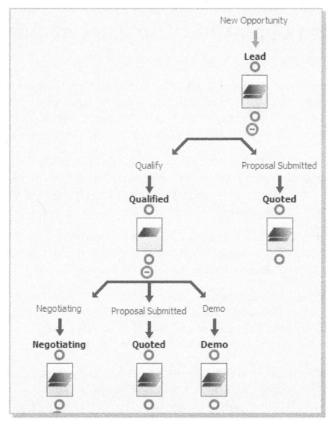

*Part of a Sales Workflow state diagram from SageCRM*

A sample sales workflow could contain the following steps:

1.  Getting a lead: This may be linked with the contact management workflow discussed previously.

2.  Qualify the lead: This is the action of confirming that the lead is a real potential customer, and that you have contact details for the customer.

3.  Call the customer: The next step may be making a phone call to the customer to attempt to make a sales meeting.

4.  Meet the customer: Following the phone call there may be a meeting to present a demo, or discuss a sale.

5. Send quote: At this stage you may need to send a quote to the customer as you get near to a sale.

6. Take order: The end of a successful sales process is the taking of the order.

Of course, the sales workflow is different for every business, which is why workflows in CRM are flexible and customizable.

# Integration opportunity for sales management

There is significant opportunity for sales management integration with ERP.

In a non-integrated CRM application opportunity management is useful, to a certain point, in the sales pipeline. Very soon, however, your sales team will want to send a quote to the customer or take an order from the customer to progress the sale. But quotes and orders are natural functions in the ERP application, not the CRM application.

This is because quotes and orders need information such as stock available, pricing, tax, and payment terms, all of which are in the ERP system and not in the CRM. Once an order is sent out, the next steps in the fulfillment cycle are shipping and invoicing, again which are in the ERP application.

The integration opportunity is to link the CRM sales opportunity business process with ERP sales quotes and sales orders business process, so that the sales user can seamlessly complete an end to end sale from within the CRM application.

Similarly, products in a non-integrated CRM application do not have inventory, or the detailed pricing that an ERP application has. (Products tend to have simple pricing in non-integrated CRM, but ERP applications can offer advanced price levels such as discounts, sale prices, bulk order discounts, and other features.)

When opportunities are integrated with sales quotes and sales orders, the line items that appear on the opportunities can be linked with ERP inventory items.

An integrated workflow means that sales users can use CRM and be linked seamlessly with sales fulfillment in the ERP.

# Workshop

Briefly outline the sales process in your business where sales are initiated and brought through to completion. Identify the teams who do this work. Outline the benefit of linking the CRM sales process with the ERP business process of quote and order creation. Are there other benefits by allowing sales users to view inventory, or any other information?

# Customer support

Customer support is another popular CRM feature. Customer support in a CRM application is for the management of customer issues. Issues could be general complaints, complaints about products such as returns, refunds or replacements, cancellations of an order, and so forth. Issues that are managed in CRM are called *cases*, or support tickets, or just tickets. Customer support can also include after sales service to ensure a good customer experience.

In a non-integrated CRM application, tickets that involve returns, refunds, or the replacement of products are not linked with the ERP inventory control system, and this makes the process disconnected. A customer support user may need to enter a ticket into the CRM application, and then they may need to go to the ERP application to process a refund, or replacement. This requires application hopping and double entry of data.

# Customer support workflow

The business process of managing customer support tickets is called the customer support workflow. Tickets are managed from initial creation through to successful or unsuccessful resolution:

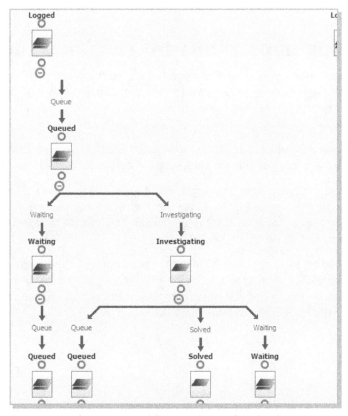

*Part of a customer workflow state diagram from SageCRM*

A typical customer support workflow may contain some or all of the following steps:

1.  **Log ticket**: A level one support user may be tasked with entering new tickets into the CRM system. Tickets may originate from e-mails sent in by the customer, or phone calls, or they may come in via another system such as a customer self- service site.

2.  **Analyze ticket**: The same support user or another more experienced support user may analyze the ticket to see whether enough information has been provided that will allow action to be taken. If there is not enough information they may have to contact the customer again to ask for more information.

3.  **Respond to the customer**: The support user may respond to the customer with additional questions, or propose a solution to the ticket. There may be a pause at this point, while waiting for the customer to respond. The ticket will be put on hold until there is a response from the customer.

4.  **Process refund, replacement, or return**: At some point in the life cycle of the ticket, it may become clear that the customer would like a refund, replacement, or return. At this point the customer user may need to go to the ERP application to continue with the workflow, necessitating application hopping and double entry of data.

5.  **Close ticket**: Finally, on successful resolution of the ticket, it is closed, and the customer support user moves on to the next ticket in the queue.

# Integration opportunity for customer support

A non-integrated CRM application is not optimal for handling customer complaints related to returning, replacing, or refunding products that have been sold, because there is no direct link between the CRM application and the ERP's inventory control or sales fulfillment process.

An ERP application is suited to recording returns, replacements, or refunds, sometimes called RMAs, but it is not suitable for managing the customer interactions.

The integration opportunity is to link up the CRM and ERP into a more seamless workflow allowing customer support to take the customer complaints using the CRM system, and then link up with the ERP system when dealing with the specifics of the returns, replacements, or refunds.

Another useful integration opportunity is to use the customer support workflow for chasing up invoices that are overdue, for delinquent accounts. In order to do that there needs to be a link between the ERP system, to get invoice information and the CRM application to handle the customer interactions.

# Workshop

Briefly outline the customer support process in your business where customer queries/ complaints are entered, and brought through to resolution. Can this process benefit by being linked with the ERP? Is there information in the ERP that is useful to a customer support person? When processing returns is it useful to have a link with ERP?

# Management information

CRM applications provide management information to allow managers and team leaders to view the progress of their teams, and to analyze their performance.

Management information usually comes in the form of easy to read visuals of the underlying data, such as charts, graphs, or lists. The information can be provided within the CRM application as dashboards, or it could be exported as reports in varying formats such as text files, CSV files, or PDF files. The following figure shows examples of some management information charts for the sales team in SageCRM:

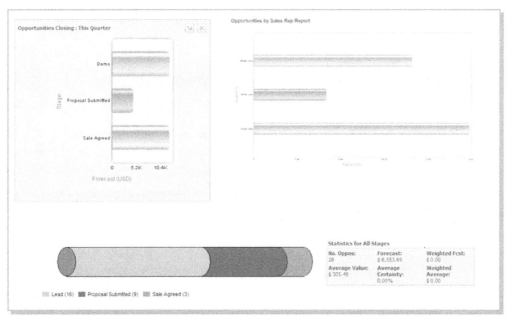

*Examples of some management information charts for the sales team in SageCRM*

In a non-integrated CRM application the information available for analysis is the information stored in the CRM application. Some examples of information that is available are:

➤ **Opportunity progress by sales user or team**: A range of charts, graphs, or reports can be made available that show the progress of opportunities grouped per user, or per sales team. The analysis may show expected revenue for the next time period, for example monthly or quarterly. They may show the quantity of opportunities or the rate that they are being processed by user or by team. This information helps the manager judge the performance of the sales team and forecast revenue.

➤ **Customer support tickets by customer support user or team**: A range of charts graphs or reports can be made available that show the progress of customer support tickets grouped per user or per customer support team. The analysis may show information such as the closure rate of tickets, or the quantity of tickets being processed, or the time taken to deal with tickets, grouped on a per user or per team basis. The information helps the manager judge the performance of the customer support team.

Information that is not available for analysis in a non-integrated CRM application is any information that resides in the ERP.

# Integration opportunity for management information

A non-integrated CRM application can show useful analysis of information that is gathered in the CRM application only. There is plenty of useful information that is stored in the ERP that will not be available.

With an integration it is possible to expand the information shown to users by adding ERP information such as order fulfillment information, invoices, purchase history, and statements. This information presented to managers and team leaders results in a more comprehensive overview and better planning.

Some examples of where adding ERP information can give a more comprehensive overview are as follows:

➤ Sales analysis: We talked about the analysis that can be done on the opportunity workflow when you have non-integrated CRM. If we add in ERP information about invoices, shipments, and other transactions, we can get a more complete analysis of a sale from the lead all the way to a shipped and delivered product. This information helps the manager judge not only how good a sales user is at making a sale, but how many of the sales are converted to revenue received and goods shipped, which is a better overall indicator of the health of the sales process.

> ➤ Customer support: We talked about the analysis that can be done on customer support tickets to see how well a customer support user or team is doing. If we add in ERP information such as data on refunds, replacements, and returns we can get a more complete analysis of a customer support ticket all the way from when it is initially logged to final resolution, even if that resolution involves an ERP workflow. The information helps the manager judge not only how good a customer support person is at closing a ticket, but how many times this results in products being returned or refunded, which gives a better overall assessment of the quality of the product or service that is being offered.

# Workshop

In general, for your customer-facing teams, managers, and team leaders, identify the ERP information that would be useful for them in analyzing their users, teams, and company performance.

# Summary

This chapter was an introductory chapter to make sure that we are all on the same page and ready to go into greater depth in later chapters. We talked about different CRM-like applications, and then we talked about some of the terminology that we will be using throughout the book. Finally, we devoted a decent amount of time to looking at the different workflows in CRM that will benefit from CRM integration.

In the section on the different CRM-like applications we talked about how as your business grows, you are more likely to need a more fully featured CRM application. In order to implement an integration, your CRM needs to have the standard CRM features, which we listed, and it also needs to be customizable and extendable.

In the section on terminology we talked about users, teams, and user roles. Users are what we call the people who use the CRM application. They are grouped into teams and the work they do is described as a role. We talked about workflow. In the integration, we will be changing the CRM workflows so that they are linked with ERP. Finally in this section, we touched on security, and how we need to make sure the data is secure.

In the latter half of the chapter, we talked about different CRM features and workflows that benefit from an integration. We talked about the benefits for contact management, sales management, customer support, and management information for managers and team leaders.

In the next chapter, we will talk about building the integration. We will cover integration architectures and concepts such as synchronization of data, and real-time views, and when to do which method. We will cover the different design areas that need to be considered when doing an integration. This will prepare us for subsequent chapters when we will get down to detailed examples of actual integration use cases.

# ≫2

# How to Implement
# an Integration

In the previous chapter, we discussed the benefits of creating an integration between CRM and ERP. We also introduced some of the terminology and concepts that will be useful for the rest of the book.

In this chapter, we will first discuss the build or buy choice, and whether it is better to purchase an out of the box integration, if one exists, or to build it yourself.

We will then explore how to implement an integration. We will do this by breaking down the components of an integration into the four main technical integration challenges. For each integration challenge we will explore solutions that have been used, and weigh up the pros and cons for each solution.

We will cover a lot of exciting new topics such as synchronization, real-time views, and screen pops. At the end of each section is a short workshop to help you understand how to apply the knowledge to your business.

By the end of this chapter, you should have a good idea of the components of an integration that need to be built, and you should have picked your preferred solutions for each component.

We will then be ready to move on to the next chapter where we will design a real-world scenario on contact integration.

## Build or buy

At this stage it is a good idea to evaluate the benefits of building your own integration against the benefits of purchasing an out-of-the-box integration, if there are out-of-the-box offerings available on the market. The choice of integrations available for your business depends on which CRM application ERP application you have.

If you have a feature-rich, customizable CRM application, then there are likely to be one or two integrations available on the market, and you should check them out as part of your initial research.

The advantages of buying an out-of-the-box integration solution are that you reduce the development risk, and in theory it should be quicker to install. The disadvantages are that you lose control over the functionality that you get, so it may not be a correct fit to your own business, or it may just be a partial fit. If it is not a fit then you may be stuck with something that does not suit your business needs.

When you build your own integration, you have control over what features you build. You can build out some or all of the use cases described in this book, depending on your business needs. You can also build on the techniques provided by this book to build out additional or different uses cases that are valuable to your business.

When you build your own integration, you have control over the schedule. You can build out basic use cases in early iterations, and then develop additional use cases in future iterations in a timeframe that suits your business.

# Workshop

In order to help you decide whether to build or buy an integration solution, do some research online for pre-built integrations available on the market for your CRM application and ERP application.

If you find out-of-the-box integration solutions that are available in your area, evaluate against your business needs:

> ➤ Are the features that they offer close enough to the features that you desire in an integration?

> ➤ Are there missing features?

> ➤ Is it possible to add new features yourself?

> ➤ How are they installed?

> ➤ How much do they cost for licensing, deployment, and ongoing support and maintenance?

# Building an integration

The building of an integration can be broken down into several design areas, or challenges that we need to solve. These high level challenges are the same for any integration with every type of ERP or CRM application.

The details of the solutions will depend on which CRM and ERP we are dealing with, which tools are available to us, and which use cases we are going to solve.

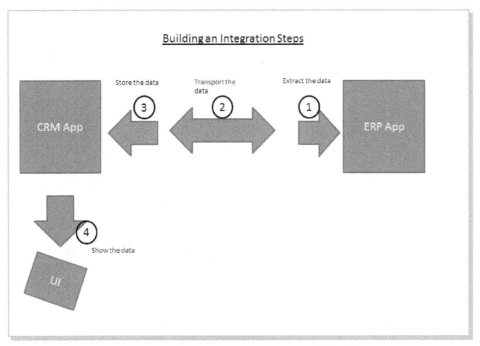

*This diagram shows the four challenges that need to be solved to build an integration*

*The challenges can be broken down into four areas:*

> **Extract the data**: Extract the data from ERP
> **Transport the data**: Transport the data between ERP and CRM
> **Store the data**: Store the data that has been extracted from ERP in CRM
> **Show the data**: Show the data in the CRM UI

# Challenge 1 – extract the data

We first need to get information out of the ERP so that we can use it in the integration. We will discuss several methods that can be used. These are:

➤ Direct access from the database

➤ Access through the business API

➤ Screen popping

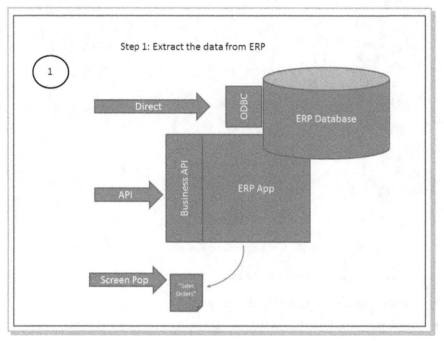

*Extracting the data from ERP, showing the different methods that can be used*

The preceding diagram gives you an illustration of where and how the data can be extracted from, but we will look at each of these methods in more detail now.

## Direct access from database

The most direct method is to go straight to the data source of the ERP, which is likely to be a database, and to extract data through the database interface. One way of doing this is by using an ODBC driver. To do this, you will need to have a username and password for accessing the database and you will need to have some knowledge of the data schema of your ERP.

If you use this method. there is an advantage of having direct access to the ERP native data, so you can get everything that is in the ERP. It can be the quickest way to get started on development.

The disadvantage is that you are bypassing the ERP business logic. Some of the data that you need may be calculated by the ERP business logic, and because you are bypassing the ERP business logic you will need to work out how to calculate it yourself. For example, the invoice balance is something that may be calculated in the ERP business logic rather than stored in the database, and sometimes the credit limit of a customer is a calculated field as well.

Some of the data may also be transformed by the ERP business logic, so you will have to look at what is shown on the ERP screens to see if there is a difference between what is shown in the UI and what is stored in the database, and make the transformation yourself. Some of the data may be spread around different schema tables. Information that is shown on an ERP UI is not necessarily stored in the same ERP schema table, so you may need to root around to find out where data is stored.

Solutions that use direct access to the database tend to use one high-level username and password that gives full database access. This is a security concern because the access that you will have is bypassing the ERP application, and will not be limited by business rules, or security checks in the application. It will be your responsibility to make sure that you do not implement anything that breaks the business logic of the ERP application. If this is a concern, you should avoid using this method.

# Access through business (API)

Most ERP applications will have some sort of business **application programming interface (API)** or indirect way of accessing data from the application. This will in fact most likely be the method that is recommended and supported by the application manufacturers, if there is a recommended and supported method.

A business API is a programmable interface through which data can be passed into and out of the ERP. The advantage of using the business API is that it will use the same business logic as the ERP user interfaces. If there are calculated fields in the ERP, they will be calculated for you. When you add data to the ERP, the same business rules are most likely to be applied as in the ERP (in some cases, they may not—you will need to check the documentation to be sure).

Other advantages of using the business API is that because it is an API that is provided for you, it should be designed to avoid issues such as database locking, user concurrency issues, or performance issues, when you use it. This is in contrast to the ODBC method where you are on your own if there are any negative impacts on the ERP.

As with the ODBC method, you will probably use one high-level username and password to access the data. However, this time you are going through the ERP application code, and you are less likely to be allowed by the application to inadvertently "break" anything in the ERP.

# Screen popping

Screen popping is not a way of accessing data, per se, but it is a way of accessing information from the ERP. Some ERPs are designed so that you can take modules such as screens, or components and launch them from outside the ERP. Because you are able to launch the screen from outside the ERP, you will be able to launch the screen from the CRM application if you want to.

A very common example of this is the ability to launch the order creation screen from outside the ERP. You could add a button to the CRM application which launches the order creation screen, and so, users of CRM would be able to create orders from within CRM.

There are obvious disadvantages to this technique. The order creation screen would look different to the CRM screens from where it was launched. Some thought needs to be put into the workflow to make it a connected user experience for the CRM user. This can be done, and is in fact discussed in more detail in the chapter on sales management integration.

We will also talk more about screen popping in the UI section of this chapter.

# Workshop

In order to help you decide how you will access your ERP, research what data access methods are available for your ERP.

Now take some time to consider the following questions:

> Do you have access to the database? Can you read and write data to the ERP database? Can you view and understand the ERP database schema?

> Is there a business API? Is there documentation or information available on how to use it? Can you read and write data through the business API?

> Does your ERP allow for components of functionality to be launched separately from the application, such as new order screens?

> Which method, direct access to the database, or access through a business API, do you favor at this time?

# Challenge 2 – transporting the data between ERP and CRM

Once we have the data out of ERP, we need to have techniques for transporting the data between the two applications.

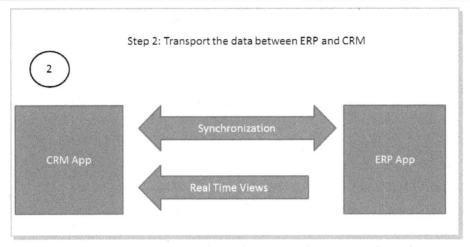

*When transporting the data between ERP and CRM there are two techniques to consider: synchronization and real-time data views*

There are two main techniques that we will explore:

➤ Synchronized data
➤ Real-time views

# Synchronized data

Synchronized data is data that is stored in ERP and also transported to CRM and stored in CRM. The data needs to be synchronized because if it changes on the ERP side it needs to be changed on the CRM side to make sure both copies stay the same, and vice versa. Synchronization is more difficult to implement than real time data views, so it should only be used when necessary.

There are two directions of synchronization:

➤ One way synchronization
➤ Bidirectional synchronization

# One way synchronization

One way synchronization is when data exists in the ERP, for example, and is copied to the CRM. The data may change in ERP, and whenever it does we need to make sure the change is copied over to CRM as well, so that both sides have the same view of the data. The data never, however, changes in CRM. Therefore, we only need to be concerned about copying the data in one direction, from ERP to CRM. We call this one way synchronization.

An example of a common one way synchronization use case is the credit limit, and credit on hold information on an A/R customer. A customer's credit limit is set in the ERP, and the credit on hold state of a customer is also set in ERP, based on the credit status of the customer at the time. It is desirable in many use cases to be able to see that information in the CRM application, as it is useful information for a sales or support user.

It would not be desirable to give the sales or support users the ability to change the credit limit or credit status. In CRM the information would be read only information, available for some users to see but not to change. This is an ideal candidate for data that is one way synchronized from ERP to CRM.

## Bidirectional synchronization

Bidirectional synchronization is when data exists in, say, the ERP, and is copied to the CRM. The data may change in the ERP, and whenever it does we need to make sure the change is copied over to CRM as well, so that both sides have the same view of the data. The data may also change in CRM, and whenever it does we need to make sure the change is copied back to ERP. We therefore need to be concerned about copying the data in both directions, from ERP to CRM and back. We call this bidirectional synchronization.

An example of a common bidirectional synchronization use case is a customer's contact information, such as phone number or email address. A customer's phone number and email address may be entered when the customer is first added to the CRM or ERP. It is also possible to change a customer's e-mail or phone information, and in fact it would a common use case for a customer to inform your business of a change of contact information.

If the customer is speaking to the sales or support users when they inform you of the new contact information, it makes sense to allow the sales or support users to enter the information directly into the CRM application and have the data copied over to the ERP. If the customer is in contact with the financial department, or a back office user, or if the customer information is being entered for the first time, it can make sense to input the contact details into the ERP and have the data copied over to the CRM. We generally would like to support the ability to copy changed phone number and e-mail information in both directions. In this case we need to bidirectionally synchronize the data.

## One way or bidirectional synchronization?

We have discussed some common examples of data that is one way synchronized or bidirectional synchronized. Other data falls into a grey area where it is not clear whether it should be one way synchronized or bidirectionally synchronized, and it comes down to business policy which option is chosen.

For example, we may decide to allow one way synchronization of a customer's name, and therefore only allow it to be changed in the ERP, or we may decide to bidirectionally synchronize a customer's name so that it can also be changed in the CRM. Other data that is open for debate is a customer's address, depending on how strict the rules are for setting the address, or a contact's name.

# Multipoint synchronization

There is also a further type of synchronization where data is copied to more than one other place, and changes are therefore copied between multiple points. This is called multipoint synchronization.

An example of this may be if data is synchronized between an ERP and a CRM, and also an e-commerce system, meaning that data has to be shared between three applications, or if you are also synchronizing with a mobile application that has a local copy of synchronized data.

This is a more complicated scenario to support, and we will not be spending much time on multi-point synchronization in our integration examples.

# Synchronization architecture options

There are several architectures used in synchronization. Your choice of architecture depends on your business needs. The two main families of synchronization architecture are:

➤ Point to point synchronization

➤ Hub and spoke synchronization

## Point to point synchronization

Point to point synchronization is the most direct way of developing a synchronization.

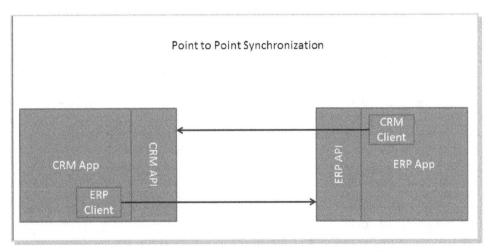

*In a point to point synchronization, client code calls the corresponding API directly*

In a point to point synchronization, when changes take place in the ERP data, this triggers CRM client software that makes the same update in the CRM data, and vice versa.

The steps involved depend on the software tools that are available for customization in the ERP and CRM, but they are something like this:

1.  Customize the ERP so that when changes take place in the ERP data, some customized code is triggered. The customized code can be regarded as CRM client code, because it will communicate with the CRM application.

    ➢ One way of doing this might be by adding triggers to the ERP database that will launch some CRM client code

    ➢ Another way to do this might be by adding customized code into the ERP UI

2.  CRM client code will authenticate with the CRM application and update the CRM data with the same changes that were made in the ERP.

For example, when a credit limit is changed in ERP, the customization could trigger some code in the ERP which will log on through the CRM business API and update the credit limit data in the CRM.

An advantage of this style of architecture is that it can support real time, or near real time synchronization of the data. When the credit limit changes in ERP, it appears to change almost immediately in the CRM application as well. This makes for nice demos, and is very satisfactory from a user experience.

There are some disadvantages to the point to point sync model because of its tightly coupled nature.

A disadvantage of this style of architecture is that when the CRM or ERP software is updated it may cause complications, for example it may be necessary to reinstall the customizations that you have made. Changes in the ERP or CRM software may mean you will need to change your ERP client software as well.

Another disadvantage due to the tight coupling is that it may sometimes slow down your ERP application, depending on how it has been implemented. For example, if your CRM client software is embedded in your ERP UI software, your user may have to wait while the update takes place. In some cases, this may be very fast and unnoticeable, but in other cases if there is a delay in the update your user may be blocked for seconds or longer. This is something that should be avoided for a good user experience.

A final disadvantage due to point to point architecture is that it does not allow very well for fault tolerance of updates. For example, if your CRM client is trying to update the credit limit in CRM, as per the preceding example, if the CRM client fails to log on to CRM, or times out, or if there is any error, then the update in CRM may fail and the data will become out of sync. Due to the point to point nature there cannot be a retry, and it will be difficult to get the data in sync again.

In some integrations, there is an option to do a full background re-sync of data, and this is put in to accommodate for situations where the data gets out of sync.

# Hub and spoke synchronization

A hub and spoke architecture is different to a point to point architecture because it has a separate component (the hub) running in between the CRM application and the ERP application (the spokes). It is called a broker, because its role is to "broker" the communication between the two applications.

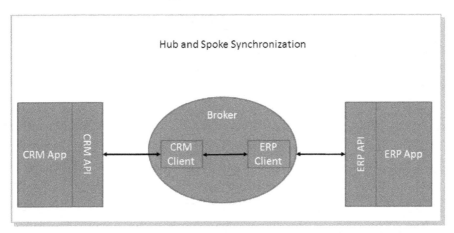

*In a hub and spoke synchronization, an external piece of software "brokers" the exchange of data between the two applications*

The broker has the ability to communicate with both the ERP and the CRM, so it has ERP client software and CRM client software contained within it. It synchronizes data between the ERP and the CRM by finding out what has changed in ERP and copying the changed data to CRM, and vice versa, by finding out what has changed in CRM and copying the changed data to ERP.

It is typically created as a windows service, running either on the ERP server or the CRM server.

The steps involved in a hub and spoke synchronization are:

1. The broker can operate on a schedule, so it can run a sync at a preset time or it can operate periodically, for example running every 5 minutes, or every hour, or once a day. It wakes up and begins the sync.

2. Inside the broker it has an ERP client, which queries the ERP for data that has changed, through the ERP API. If there is data that has changed, the ERP client will get a copy of the data.

3. The broker will pass the data to the CRM client, and the data will be transformed to the way that CRM expects it.

4. The CRM client will connect to CRM and update the data in the CRM database.

5. The broker then performs steps 2 to 4 but in the opposite direction.

# How to detect what data has changed

Change detection is one of the challenges of the hub and spoke method of synchronization. Periodically, the broker will initiate a request to the ERP application to determine what data has changed since the last time a synchronization took place. How does it know what data has changed?

One way to detect what data has changed is if the ERP has timestamps on each record in the database that are updated every time the record changes. If the broker keeps the timestamp of the last time that it did a sync, it can request all the data with a timestamp after the timestamp of the last sync. This is the easiest way to do it, and if your ERP does this you are very lucky.

For example, if the ERP has timestamps at a field level, and you are synchronizing customer credit limits you could query the ERP for any customer credit limits that have changed since the last sync, and pass them on to the CRM application.

Or if the ERP only has timestamps at a record level, you could query the ERP for customer records that have changed since the last synch, and pass the entire customer records on to the CRM application as updated records.

If the ERP does not have timestamps, and many do not, then you need to think of another way to determine what has changed.

An alternative way to detect what data has changed is for the broker to keep a local copy of all the data that it is synchronizing. When the broker does the next sync it gets a new copy of all the data that it is synchronizing, and compares it with the local copy. Any data that is different has by definition changed, and this will then be passed on to the CRM as changed data.

For example, if you are synchronizing A/R customers from the ERP to CRM. The broker will keep a local copy of the A/R customers. When it is doing a new sync it will request all the A/R customers from the ERP and compare them with the local copy of the A/R customers. Any A/R customers that are different have been updated, and they are passed on to the CRM application.

This is a very time consuming solution. One way to speed it up is to use hash keys. Instead of storing complete copies of each A/R customer record, store a hash key of the record. At the next sync get the A/R customers from ERP and convert them to hash keys, and compare the hash keys with the local hash keys. Again, if the hash key has changed it means the record has changed, and any changed records can be passed to the CRM as updated records.

If change detection is too difficult, the final worst option is to update all the data every time there is a sync.

For example, if you are synchronizing A/R customers from ERP to CRM, and you simply cannot do any form of change detection, every time there is a sync you will need to request all the A/R customer records from ERP and send them over to the CRM, overwriting the CRM customer records.

This is very inefficient, and can be intensive on the servers. Generally, if you are doing this method you would make the synchronization cycles infrequent, perhaps once a day, or once a week, outside office hours. If you do not have change detection it means that you can only do one way sync. You will be able to copy data from ERP to CRM, but because you are overwriting the customer data in CRM every time, you will not be able to allow the data to change in CRM. Any changes in CRM will get overwritten.

However, if you are OK with running the sync once a day or once a week, and not allowing changes to the data in CRM, this last brute force method is worth considering.

## Conflict resolution

Rules for conflict resolution need to be considered when you are doing bidirectional synchronization. A conflict may occur if you have data that can change in both ERP and CRM, in one sync cycle. When the next synch takes place, one of the changes will need to be overwritten by the other change, otherwise the data will get out of sync.

For example, if you are allowing e-mail addresses to be changed in both ERP and CRM, a user may change an e-mail address in CRM, and another user may change the same e-mail address in ERP. When the next sync takes place, which user's change will be overwritten?

The rules for conflict resolution could be based on date, so that the last user who made the change wins, or the first user who made the change wins, or they could be based on application, such as the change in the CRM application wins, or the change in the ERP application wins. In my experience the most common conflict resolution rule is that the change in the ERP application wins because the ERP is regarded as having the more reliable data.

Note that this issue occurs in the hub and spoke synchronization scenario because it is most likely not in real time, and the synchronization only takes place periodically.

## Advantages and disadvantages of hub and spoke architecture

The advantages of having an outside broker to manage the synchronization process are that the synch is decoupled from the internals of the CRM and the ERP. As long as you use supported application APIs to connect to the ERP and CRM, it should be much easier to upgrade both the CRM and the ERP without having to make any changes to your software in the broker.

The hub and spoke methods allow for better fault tolerance and error handling. If, for example, there is an error connecting to either of the applications, or a timeout, the broker could be configured to try again later. The data will eventually be synchronized.

The broker runs behind the scenes, and not from within a user's UI, and therefore there should be no impact on the users who are using the system, either by experiencing slowness in their UIs, or by seeing any strange messages about synchronization.

The disadvantages are that the brokers tend to not update data in real time. As they run on a scheduled or periodic basis, there is a time lag between data changing in the ERP, and appearing in CRM. This time lag could be a second, an hour, a day, or a week, depending on the broker and the implementation.

One way to mitigate the time lag is to find a way to trigger a synchronization from within the application, for example if data changes in the ERP. If there is a way for the ERP to send a message to the broker that the data has changed, the broker can "wake up" and run an immediate synchronization. If it does this it will greatly reduce the time lag between data changing in one application and the other.

## Vector clock synchronization

The hub and spoke architecture that we have talked about so far has been for synchronization between two applications. In more complex scenarios where you are synchronizing between more than two applications there is a synchronization design that is very powerful called vector clock synchronization.

An example of when you may have an integration with more than two applications could be if you are integrating your ERP with a CRM application and another application such as an e-commerce website. It may be possible to change a customer's e-mail address or telephone information in the ERP, the CRM, and the e-commerce applications at the same time.

Vector clock synchronization uses a concept of ticks to store the version of every record at every application in the synchronization. The broker passes the ticks between the different applications, to determine whether a record has changed. This is used to decide whether data needs to be copied from a newer version to another application that has an older version of the data. Eventually the data in all the applications are brought up to the same version. Vector clock sync allows for conflict resolution rules and has a range of variants to satisfy different multi-point scenarios.

It is a more complex solution than we need for our point to point integration, but if you are doing a multipoint integration or plan to do one in the future, it is worth considering from the start of your implementation because it is easier to design it in from the start rather than having to bring it in at a later stage.

# Real time data views

Real time data views are views of ERP data that are read and viewed in the CRM UI. The data is never edited or changed in the CRM UI, and no copy of the data is stored in the CRM database.

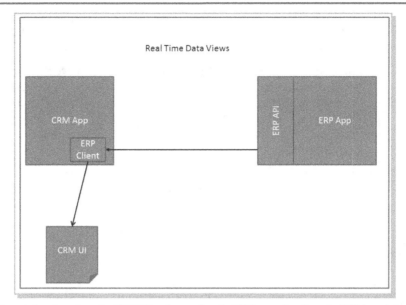

*In real time data views the CRM UI makes a call to the ERP to get data from the ERP in real time*

The use case for real time data views is for when you would like to view data in the ERP that is not strongly connected with a business process in CRM, and when the data is not going to be changed in CRM. In this case, there is no need to synchronize the data so that there is a local copy in the CRM database. It is fine to just read the data directly from the ERP, and show it in the CRM UI.

For example, it may be desirable to look at a customer's purchase history. This information would be useful for a sales user making a phone call to a customer about a new sale. It is not information that is tightly tied up with a CRM business process, and you do not want the sales user to be able to change the purchase history data. This is a good example of something that could be used in a real time data view.

Other examples of data that make good real-time views in some cases are pricing information, invoice information, refunds, receipts, or inventory information, or in general, customer information and transactions for the later part of the sales cycle after quotes and orders.

The way real time data views are implemented is by adding UI controls to the CRM UI which connect to the ERP data source rather than the CRM data source:

1. Choose where you want to launch the real time data view. If it is data specific to a customer you may want to launch it from within the customer area of the application. If it is more general data you may want to launch it from a main menu or top context area.

2. Add a new list control or screen control to the CRM UI that will be used to display the real time data.

3. When the new list or screen is launched, it needs to trigger custom code that will connect to the ERP API, collect the data from the ERP, and add the data to the CRM list or screen.

   ➤ In order to connect to the ERP API it will need to have the correct authentication information. This will depend on the implementation, but care needs to be taken to not hardcode the username and password into the customized code. This will be a security breach, and also, if the password ever changes, the feature will be unable to connect any more until the code is changed.

   ➤ The code needs to collect the data from ERP. If the data is related to an ERP customer you will need to pass the ERP customer reference.

   ➤ Add the ERP data to the custom control.

## Workshop

Consider some of the grey areas for one way synchronization and bidirectional synchronization, such as customer name sync and address sync. Based on what you know now, would you make them one way synchronization or bidirectional?

Given any tools provided by the software manufacturer, consider how easy it will be to monitor the synchronization process, and how you will handle error conditions.

Consider the advantages and disadvantages of the different synchronization methods that were discussed. Which is most suited to your business needs—point to point synchronization, or hub and spoke synchronization? Weigh up the different attributes of the different sync methods:

- ➤ How important is the real time update of data to you?
- ➤ How important is fault tolerance and error handling?
- ➤ How much time and skills do you have to invest in synchronization?
- ➤ Do the CRM and ERP customization APIs favor one method over the other?

Consider the advantages and disadvantages of synchronization of data versus real time view data. Investigate your ERP to see if it will support the real time data view architecture.

## Challenge 3 – storing the data in CRM

In some cases, it is suitable to store the data in CRM, and in some cases it is not. We have talked in the previous sections about synchronization of data, where the data will be stored in the CRM database, and real time data views where the data will not be stored in the CRM database.

# How to store the data in CRM

If your CRM application has the ability to be customized and extended it will be possible to store your ERP data in the CRM database. The methods for extending the database will be different for each CRM application.

Typically, for smaller changes such as adding new fields to the customer entity, there may be some simple customization tools available that will allow you to customize your CRM UI and will add the new fields to the database at the same time.

For bigger changes such as adding new tables to the CRM database to support new entities you may need to do some more advanced customization, and there is more likely to be some coding involved.

There may be point and click customization tools for all the database changes that you wish to make, or there may be an element of coding for all the database changes you wish to make; it depends on the CRM application.

## Guidelines for deciding when to store data in the CRM database

There are some questions that you can ask about your integration that will help you determine whether or not you should be storing the data in the CRM database.

|  | Data is part of a CRM entity | Data is not part of a CRM entity but is used in a CRM business process | Data is not part of a non CRM entity and is not used in a CRM business process |
|---|---|---|---|
| To store or not to store in CRM? | Store data in CRM database. | Store data in CRM database. | No need to store the data in CRM database. |

## Is the data part of a CRM entity?

When the data is closely embedded with CRM entities it is usually better to store the data in CRM.

For example, a common use case in integrations is to show the customer credit limit in the CRM UI. The customer entity already exists in CRM, but it does not have a credit limit field. In the UI, it is most likely that the credit limit field will be added to the customer screen.

Because the customer screen already exists in CRM, and because the screen is populated with data from the CRM database, it makes sense to add the credit limit to the CRM database, in the same location as the other customer data.

Another example of this is customer phone numbers or e-mail addresses. We have discussed before that e-mail addresses and phone numbers are typical examples of data that are likely to be edited in both the CRM application and the ERP application.

E-mail address and phone number screens already exist in CRM, and may not need to be changed to be able to show ERP-sourced e-mail addresses and phone numbers. The storage location of the e-mail addresses and phone numbers should be in the CRM database.

## Is the data not part of a CRM entity but used in a CRM business process?

Sometimes the data that is involved in an integration is not tightly connected to any existing CRM entities. For example a sales order or sales quote is not always part of a standalone CRM application, because some CRM applications have a different entity called opportunities. If a sales order or sales quote is part of your CRM application, then part 1 applies and you should store them in your CRM database anyway.

If you are improving your standalone CRM sales business process, or workflow, you are likely to consider adding sales quotes and sales orders to the workflow, even though they are not normally full entities within a CRM application. We will talk about this a lot more in the chapter on sales management integration.

In order to bring ERP sales quotes and sales orders into your sales business process you can synchronize your ERP sales orders and sales quotes to the CRM database, and/or allow for the creation of sales orders and quotes in the CRM database and synchronize them back to the ERP. You will need to store the sales orders and sales quotes in your CRM database.

## Is the data only loosely associated with a CRM business process, and is it read only?

When the data is only loosely associated with a CRM business process and it is read only, it is simpler to not store the data in CRM.

An example of data that is loosely associated with a CRM business process would be an ERP price list. A price list taken from the ERP is useful for a sales person if they are answering questions from a customer on pricing. The information normally resides in the ERP, but it can be taken from the ERP and displayed in CRM as part of the integration.

The way it could be added to CRM is by having a button that launches a screen that contains the price list information.

An ERP price list is loosely coupled with a CRM business process because it is typically not vital information to any of the workflows—the price list information does not need to be embedded in any of the native CRM entities and it does not result in a change to an existing CRM workflow. It is a standalone feature.

An ERP price list is also read only in CRM. You would typically not want your CRM users to be able to change an ERP price list. It should be an exact copy of the price list information in ERP.

In the case of data like ERP price lists, there is no advantage in storing the data in CRM, and it is preferable to treat the data as a real time view rather than synchronized data. Real time views are easier to maintain than synchronized data because you do not have to be concerned with changing the CRM database, or keeping the data up to date in two different places over time.

If there are technical difficulties with implementing real time views, the fallback position is to synchronize the data.

## Workshop

Investigate your CRM application to find out how to add data to the CRM database:

> ➤ Are there tools and software development kits available?

> ➤ How much of the work is point and click, and how much of it is more complex customization?

> ➤ Is it tied to the UI customization abilities of your CRM application?

# Challenge 4 – displaying the data in CRM UI

After all our backend work, we finally need to do the most visible part to the user, which is to show the information that we have in the CRM UI so that it can be used by our CRM users.

The way to customize your CRM UI depends on which CRM application you have. The CRM application should come with tools and instructions to help you make the changes.

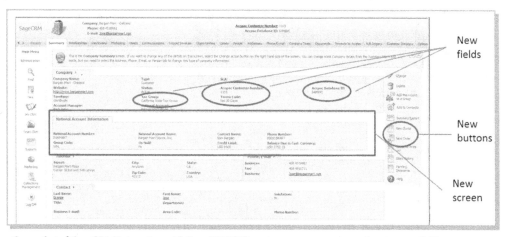

*Screenshot of SageCRM integration with Sage ERP 300, customer summary screen showing new fields, new screen, and new buttons*

The screenshot shows a SageCRM customer area which has been customized in an integration with Sage ERP 300. In the screenshot, you can see several different types of customization, new fields, a new screen, and new buttons.

In general, the types of changes that need to be made are:

> ➤ Adding fields to screens or lists
>
> ➤ Adding new screens or lists
>
> ➤ Adding new buttons to launch other features
>
> ➤ Adding new CRM reports or dashboards

# Adding fields to screens or lists

Some data that is synchronized from ERP to CRM can be added to an existing screen or list in CRM. For example, if you bring over customer information from the ERP such as credit limit, tax group, or payment terms, you can add that information to an existing customer screen.

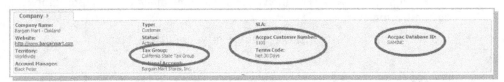

*SageCRM integration with Sage ERP 300, customer summary screen showing close up of new fields*

The screenshot shows a close up of the SageCRM integrated with Sage ERP 300 customer summary screen, showing additional ERP information added in new fields: **Tax Group**, **Customer Number**, **Terms Code (Payment Terms)**, and the **ERP Database ID**.

# Adding new screens or lists

You may be synchronizing data that does not fit naturally into an existing screen or list in CRM, and which may fit better in a new screen or list.

The following screenshot is a close up of the SageCRM to Sage ERP 300 customer summary screen showing a section that is a new screen. The information shown is the national account details of the customer.

*SageCRM integration with Sage ERP 300, customer summary screen showing close up of new screen*

National accounts can be thought of like a head office for a group of customers. Several customers can have the same national account, or head office, meaning they can be grouped together for purchasing and invoicing.

In this example, the national account data is taken from the ERP as a real time view, but it could also be synchronized data. This does not affect how it is shown in the UI.

New screens and lists can also be displayed as pop-ups. We will talk more about pop ups in the section on adding new buttons.

You may, of course, also want to add new lists. Some examples of adding a new list may be if you are adding sales quotes, sales orders, or sales invoices to the integration. These transactions would usually be shown as a list of quotes, orders, or invoices. You may then be able to drill down on a record in the list to see the full summary. We will talk more about lists of quotes, orders, and invoices, in the chapter on implementing the sales management integration.

When adding a list, there are some things that you need to think about before you start that you do not need to think about for a screen:

> ➤ If you are implementing a list, take care to think about what happens when you have long lists that exceed the length of the page. If you are using a list control this may be taken care of, but if you are implementing your own hand built list you will need to think about a paging mechanism.

> ➤ If you are implementing a list, think also about ways of filtering the list. Do you want to show all the information or a subset, and do you want to allow your user to filter the data? For example if you are showing invoices, returns, or receipts, you may want to be able to filter them by a date range, or by paid status.

# Adding new buttons to launch other features

Buttons are useful customization tools because they can used to launch new UI components. They can launch new screens, new lists, or even new applications. When buttons are used to launch new screens that pop up from the CRM application, we call them screen pops:

*SageCRM integration with Sage ERP 300, customer summary screen showing close up of customized buttons that launch new screens and screen pops*

The screenshot is a close-up of the SageCRM to Sage ERP 300 customer summary screen showing new buttons that have been added for the integration.

The **New Quote** and the **New Order** buttons launch new screens that are components of the Sage ERP 300 application, and are used to create new quotes and orders.

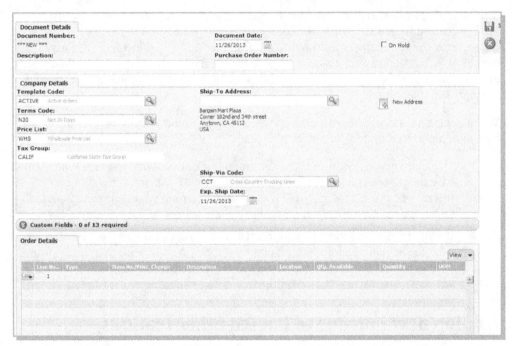

*SageCRM integration with Sage ERP 300, order entry screen that is a pop up of a Sage ERP 300 screen*

When a user clicks on the **New Order** button, for example, they are brought to a screen that is not a native CRM UI component, but that is a Sage ERP 300 UI component, launched from CRM. The user can use the component to enter a new order directly into Sage ERP 300.

In this way, the user is able to use the CRM application for their sales workflow, and when it comes to taking an order, they do not need to leave the CRM application. The launching of the new order screen is from within the CRM workflow, even though the order is actually created in the ERP application.

Another example of a screen pop is with the SageCRM integration with Sage ERP 100.

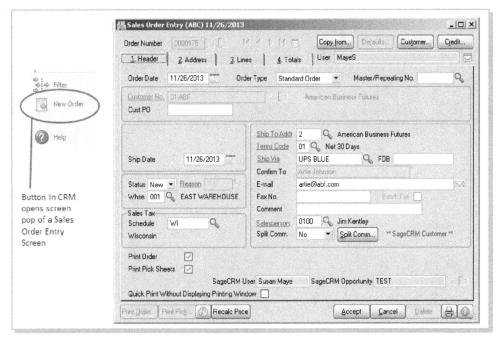

*SageCRM integration with Sage ERP 100 sales order entry screen, which is a screen pop from SageCRM*

This screenshot shows a similar use case with a different ERP application. In this example, the user, again, has a **New Order** button in the CRM UI. When they click the button a new component is launched, which is the sales order entry screen for Sage ERP 100. Using this screen, the user enters the order directly into the Sage ERP 100 application.

The look and feel of this example is very different to the look and feel of the Sage ERP 300 example. That is because the technologies used in building the components are different. The component for Sage ERP 300 was built with Java technology, and the component for Sage ERP 100 was built with Windows technology. Even though they look different, the workflow for the user is the same.

You may be thinking, why use screen pops—why not build the screens in the CRM UI? Screen pops tend to be used for use cases where the components already exist in ERP, and where it would be a lot of work to rebuild them in CRM. The order entry screen is a good example. A "new order" screen in ERP takes many years of development effort to build, and it would be a big project to rewrite some or all of those rules in CRM. The quicker option is to launch the screen pop of a "new order" component from CRM and reuse the work that somebody else has already done. We will talk more about this in the sales management integration chapter.

The other example of adding new buttons is to launch screens or lists that are real time views of ERP data. Some examples of views of real time data shown on the SageCRM integration with Sage ERP 300 customer summary screen are customer price lists, customer sales history, and pending shipments. When the user clicks on the button they get a screen pop of a real time data view of the ERP information.

*SageCRM integration with Sage ERP 300 Customer Price List real time view, which is a screen pop from the customer summary screen*

For example, if they click on the **Customer Price List** button, they will get a screen pop of the price list for the customer, which is taken from the ERP as a real time view.

# Adding CRM reports or dashboards

We talked in the previous chapter about how a CRM to ERP integration gives managers and team leaders greater access to information, which they can use to analyze the performance of their business.

The way to provide the improved management information is by adding new CRM reports and dashboards to the application that show the new data that has been added with the integration.

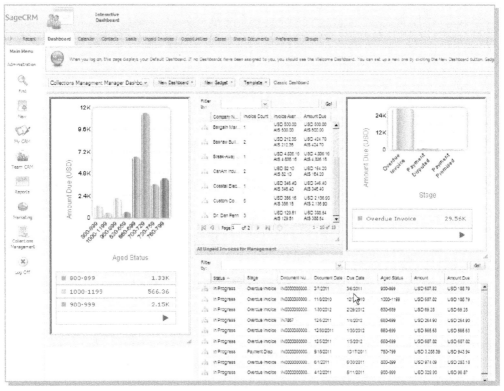

*SageCRM integrated with Sage ERP 300 collections management dashboard showing graphs, lists, and summaries related to overdue invoices*

An example of a new dashboard could be a dashboard that shows information about overdue invoices. This could be used as part of a collections management integration module. The screenshot above shows a SageCRM integration with Sage ERP 300, dashboard for managers, containing graphs, lists, and summary information related to overdue invoices. This information would not be available in a standalone CRM application.

*SageCRM integrated with Sage ERP 300 screenshot of an* **"All Customers Who Owe Money"** *report*

An example of a new report that could be added to a CRM integration is one that shows a list of customers with overdue invoices. This can be used by managers to direct sales teams to chase up the invoices. The preceding screenshot shows a report from a SageCRM integration with Sage ERP 300, showing a report of customers who owe money to the business, and how much money they owe. This information would not be available in a standalone CRM application.

We will talk more about this report and dashboard example in the chapter on collections management integration.

# Workshop

Investigate your CRM application to find out how to customize the CRM UI:

> How do you add fields to screens or lists?

> How do you add new screens or lists?

> How do you add buttons, or any other launching mechanism, to launch screen pops and real time views?

> How do you add or edit dashboards and reports?

# Summary

In this chapter, we have talked about the different challenges in implementing a CRM integration with ERP. The details of the solution will be different for every CRM and ERP application, but the high level challenges are always the same.

We broke the challenges into technical areas, to make it easier to explain, giving several solutions for each technical area, and weighing up the advantages and disadvantages of each solution. The challenges were divided into discussions of how to:

> Extract the data from ERP

> Transport the data between ERP and CRM

> Store the data in CRM database

> Display the data in the CRM UI

In the *Extract the data from ERP* section, we covered the different methods that can be used to read data from the ERP. Direct database access may be the simplest, but there are drawbacks because it bypasses the business logic. Using the business API, if there is one available, is the preferred option. We also introduced the concept of screen pops, which will be an important tool in our arsenal of development options.

In the section about transporting data between ERP and CRM, we talked about synchronization, both one way sync and bidirectional sync. We compared the two synchronization architectures of point to point, and hub and spoke. Point to point allows for real time updates, but is not very fault tolerant. Hub and spoke is more fault tolerant, but it sometimes leads to delays in data sync. We also talked about real time data views, a preferred method for simpler use cases.

In the *Store the data in CRM* section, we talked about the need to change the CRM schema to store additional ERP data. How to do this is dependent on the CRM customization tools that are available.

Finally, in the *Display the data in the CRM UI* section, we covered the different types of CRM customization that we will be doing: adding fields to screens or lists, adding screens or lists, adding buttons for screen pops, or real time views, and adding new dashboards and reports for the management of information.

In the next chapter, we will do a real-world scenario of a contacts integration. We will go through some use cases for a sample company to go through the design of the integration, step by step. In later chapters we will do even more integration scenarios.

# $>3$

# How to Build a Contact Integration

The earlier chapters were focused on covering the background information needed for building an integration between CRM and ERP. In the first chapter we talked about the business benefits of building an integration, and we introduced some of the terminology that we use throughout the book. In the next chapter, we talked about the high level architecture of an integration, and we weighed up the pros and cons of the different approaches that are available.

From this chapter on, we will go into the detailed design of integration features. The first integration feature will be contact management integration, which we will cover in this chapter.

We will talk about the use cases of the contact integration, using an example based on a real-world scenario of a fictional company, **RideRight Bike Parts**. We will take the use cases and convert them to new integration workflows that we will need to support. We will then design the solution using techniques such as entity diagrams, entity mapping, field mapping, and so on.

As this is the first chapter to design integration functionality, we will also explain the design concepts that we use as we go along so that they can be repeated for the integration features that we discuss in later chapters.

# Contact management integration scenario

The RideRight Bike Parts company is based in Vancouver, British Columbia. It is an importer and wholesaler of specialized bicycle parts from manufacturers in Asia. It focuses on specialized bicycle accessories, for example: bicycle saddles, handles, bicycle bells, drink holders, baskets, locks, brakes, tires, wheels, puncture repairs kits, and bicycle pumps.

RideRight sells the specialized bike parts to bicycle shops, and direct to individuals by mail, throughout British Columbia and the rest of Canada.

RideRight has a sales team that makes sales to the bike shops, and chases leads. The Sales Director in RideRight purchases the leads from bike clubs, and bike-related event organizers throughout Canada.

RideRight already has an ERP application and a CRM application, but they are not integrated. This has led to disconnects in their business processes.

1.  The RideRight sales users process leads and enter them into CRM. When the leads are qualified they need to remember to put them into the ERP application as well. Sometimes, they forget to do this, and this has led to problems taking orders because the customer details are in CRM but not in the ERP. They would like to have all their qualified CRM customers in ERP.

2.  RideRight have had the ERP system for many years, but they only purchased CRM in the last two years. There are several thousand customers in the ERP application from the pre-CRM days that have not been entered into the CRM application. When doing a marketing campaign they currently can only target the recent customers who have been entered in CRM. They would like to have all their ERP customers in CRM, so that they can run marketing campaigns with all their customers.

3.  When customers change their contact information they inform the sales users. The sales users try to remember to update both the CRM application and the ERP application with the changes, but sometimes they forget to update both applications, some users are new, or poorly trained, and only update one application, and occasionally they make a mistake and update the CRM application with different details to the ERP application. The sales director knows that many customers' contact information in CRM is different to their contact information in ERP. They would like to have the same contact information in both systems.

4.  When sales users are communicating with their customers, and negotiating a sale, they occasionally need to know what the customer's credit limit and payment terms are, whether the customer is on credit hold, and sometimes it is useful to check their tax information. This information is stored in the ERP. To get the information they send an e-mail request to a member of the accounting department, which can take hours or a day or more. They would like to have the information available to hand in the CRM application.

RideRight have identified that a contacts integration between CRM and ERP will resolve disconnects in their business process. They have identified new business process workflows in CRM that will define how the changes will improve their users' experience.

# Integration workflows

The use cases that are required for RideRight can be converted into new integration workflows that need to be implemented; the following figure indicates how this may be done:

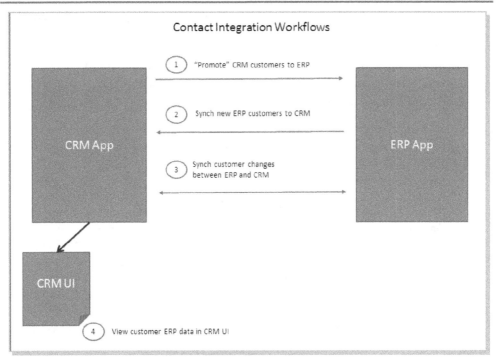

*Integration workflows for the contact integration*

The new workflows are as follows:

> ➤ The ability to promote CRM customers to ERP
> ➤ The synchronization of ERP customers from ERP to CRM
> ➤ The ability to view ERP customer information on CRM customer screens

## Promoting CRM customers to ERP

When leads are converted to customers in CRM, they need to be re-entered in ERP. The workflow will be changed in CRM so that there will be an easy way to automatically copy the customer information from CRM to ERP. This will only be for qualified CRM customers, those that are regarded as good enough to be synchronized to ERP. It will be a manually triggered action. A user in CRM will manually select a customer to be "promoted" to ERP by clicking on a button or some other action.

# Automatic synchronization of ERP customers from ERP to CRM

When customers are entered into ERP they need to be manually re-entered into CRM. The workflow will be changed so that customers in ERP will be synchronized to CRM. This is broken down into several sub features:

> **New customer synch**: When new customers are added to ERP they need to be re-entered in CRM. The workflow will be changed so that new customers in ERP will be automatically synchronized to CRM.

> **Bulk import of customers**: There are already several thousand customers in ERP that are not in CRM. A feature will be made available to allow all customers in ERP to be imported in bulk to CRM in one go. This will be used as a one-off feature to copy all the ERP customer information to CRM, and to ensure that all the ERP customer information is the same in both ERP and CRM. The bulk copy will be made a repeatable feature so that in the event of major change such as an ERP database restore or an error occurring where the customer data in ERP becomes out of synch with the customer data in CRM, it will be possible to re-run the bulk import, to make sure that the ERP data matches the CRM data.

> **Synch of customer updates**: When customer information changes, the sales users need to input the changes in both CRM and ERP. The workflow will be changed so that the synchronization feature will synchronize updates, so that changes in customer information in CRM will be synchronized with ERP.

This means that sales users will only need to change customer information in one place, either CRM or ERP, and the change will be synchronized to the other app.

## Viewing ERP customer information on CRM customer screens

When a sales user wants to see some customer information that only exists in ERP such as credit limit or payment terms, they need to ask the accounting department for the information. The workflow will be changed so that they can see this financial information immediately on the CRM UI.

# Designing the integration

We have defined the workflows that need to be implemented. The next thing we need to do is to design the contact integration. The design of the integration involves several steps:

> Step 1: Create entity diagrams
> Step 2: Map the entity diagrams
> Step 3: Define the unique identifiers
> Step 4: Define the fields and field mappings
> Step 5: Define the CRUD rules

As this is the first time we are designing an integration feature, each step will include an explanation of the step, followed by a worked example. The worked example will use the real-world applications of SageCRM and Sage ERP 300, just so that it is realistic. In the workshops you will be asked to do the corresponding design steps for your CRM and ERP.

# Step 1 – entity diagrams

The first step is to do entity diagrams of the data that you are working with.

An entity diagram is a diagram is a graphical representation of entities and their relationships with each other. For us, an entity is concept that defines a logical partition of the data that we will be working with. We need to draw entity diagrams for the CRM data and the ERP data.

A worked example will help explain what we need to do. We know that we are syncing customer information, and so we need to draw an entity diagram of customers for both CRM and ERP.

## Entity diagram for SageCRM customers

Here is an entity diagram for SageCRM customers, followed by an explanation:

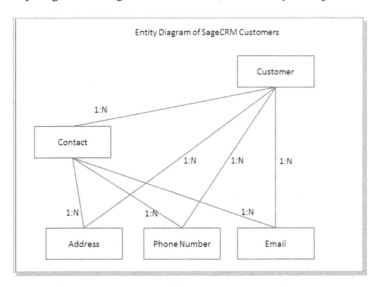

The explanation of this graph is that every box represents an entity in SageCRM. In SageCRM each entity is stored in a separate database table. The customer information that we are interested in is stored in five entities, there is customer information, contact information, address, phone number, and e-mail information. The contact, address, phone number, and e-mail entities are sub-entities of the customer entity. We say that the customer is a "parent", and each sub entity is a "child" of the customer.

Each line represents a relationship, which is a "has" relationship. Each line has a "number, colon, number" beside it. This combination defines how many of the first entity "has" of the second entity. "N" means many.

Taken together, for example, we see a line between customer and contact, with the 1: N combination. This means that a customer "has" many contacts, or when you are adding a customer in SageCRM you can add as many contacts to the customer as you wish.

Or, for example, we see a line between contact and address, with the 1: N combination. This means that a contact "has" many contacts, or when you are adding a contact to SageCRM you can associate as many addresses with the contact as you wish.

In SageCRM, the previous diagram explains that you can add as many contacts as you wish to a customer, and you can add as many addresses, phone numbers, and e-mail addresses as you wish to a contact or a customer.

# Entity diagram for Sage ERP 300 customers

The next thing you need to do is an entity diagram for the ERP customers. Here is an entity diagram for Sage ERP 300 customers followed by an explanation:

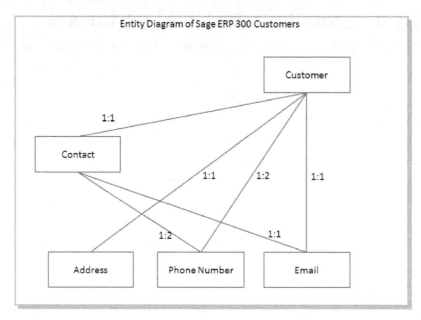

In the entity diagram of Sage 300 ERP customers, there are many similarities with the CRM entity diagram. The entities are the same: customers, contacts, addresses, phone numbers, and e-mail addresses.

There are also several differences. This time a customer has only 1 contact and not many contacts. A contact has only 1 e-mail address, and 2 phone numbers, and not many e-mail addresses and phone numbers. A contact does not have an address.

In summary, a customer has one contact and one address. A customer and a contact have two phone numbers and one e-mail address each.

Once the entity diagrams are complete, we can move on to the next step, which is to work out how the CRM entity diagram and the ERP entity diagram will map to each other.

# Workshop

Create an entity relationship diagram for customers for your CRM application. Include contacts, addresses, phone numbers, and e-mail addresses. Capture the parent-child relationships and the 1: N relationships for each sub entity.

Create an entity relationship diagram for customers for your ERP application. Include contacts, addresses, phone numbers, and e-mail addresses. Capture the parent-child relationships and the 1: N relationships for each sub entity.

# Step 2 – mapping the entity diagrams to each other

The entity diagrams for CRM customers and ERP customers are not the same. We will be synchronizing CRM customers and ERP customers with each other, so we need to work out how we will deal with the differences in the entity relationships. We need to define a mapping between the CRM entities and the ERP entities.

We will do a worked example of a mapping for SageCRM customer entities to Sage ERP 300 entities. In the workshop you will need to do the mapping for your CRM customer entities to your ERP customer entities.

# Entity mapping

The goal of this exercise is to define rules for the mapping of the entities between CRM and ERP to resolve the issue that that the entity relationships for CRM and ERP are different.

# Customers

An ERP customer can map one to one with a CRM customer. A CRM customer will not necessarily map to an ERP customer because not all CRM customers are synchronized with ERP, only qualified CRM customers are synchronized. We need to distinguish the customers in CRM that are synchronized to ERP and those that are not. The following screenshot shows SageCRM integration with Sage ERP 300. Customers have a "type" field. Customers of "type = Customer" are synchronized with ERP. Customers with any other type are not synchronized:

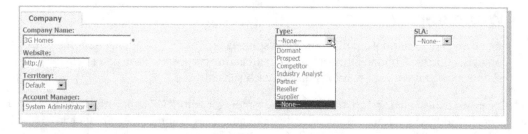

The technique that we shall use in this example is to assume that there is a customer type field in the CRM application and we will use the customer type field in CRM to differentiate the CRM customers. We shall create a rule that customers of type "ERP customer" will be synchronized with ERP. CRM customers of any other type will not be synchronized.

# Contacts

A CRM customer can have many contacts, but an ERP customer can only have one. This means that many of the contacts in CRM will not be synchronized with ERP:

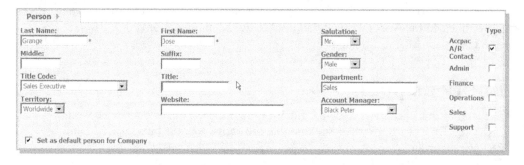

Again, let's assume for this example that there is a contact type field in the CRM application and use the contact type field to identify the contacts that are synchronized. The first rule will be that any CRM contacts of type "ERP contact" will be synchronized with ERP and CRM contacts of any other type will not be synchronized. Only some CRM customers are synchronized so we need to define a second rule that only CRM customers of type "ERP customer" can have a contact of type "ERP contact".

Finally, as only one CRM contact per customer can be synchronized, we need to define a third rule, which is that for every customer of type "ERP customer" there must be one, and only one contact of type "ERP contact".

# Address

Both CRM customers and contacts can have many addresses but an ERP customer can only have one address and an ERP contact has no addresses:

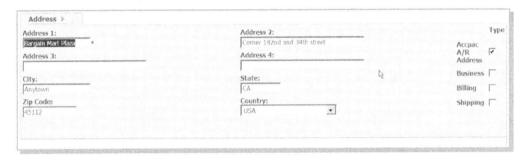

Let's again assume that there is an address type field in the CRM application and use address types to identify which addresses in CRM are synchronized. The rules will be: only addresses of type "ERP Address" will be synchronized, only CRM customers of type "ERP customer" can have an address of type "ERP Address", and finally for every CRM customer of type "ERP customer" there must be one and only one address of type "ERP Address".

# Phone number

Both CRM customers and contacts can have as many phone numbers as they wish, but ERP customers and contacts can only have two phone numbers each. If we change CRM so that it can only have two phone numbers per customer or contact, it will match the ERP entity relationship. Let's define a rule that CRM will be customized to only have two phone numbers per customer and contact.

# E-mail address

Both CRM customers and contacts can have as many e-mail addresses as needed, but ERP customers and contacts can only have one e-mail address. If we change CRM so that it can only have one e-mail address per customer or contact, it will match the ERP entity relationship. Let's define a rule that CRM will be customized so that it only allows one e-mail address per customer or contact.

# Summary of entity mapping

The summary of our discussion on entity mappings is contained in the following table:

| Entity | Mapping rule |
|---|---|
| Customer | CRM customers of type "ERP customer" will be synchronized with ERP customers. |
| Contact | CRM contacts of type "ERP contact" will be synchronized with ERP contacts. There must be one, and only one, CRM contact of type "ERP contact" per customer of type "ERP customer". |
| Address | CRM addresses of type "ERP address" will be synchronized with ERP addresses. There must be one, and only one, CRM address of type "ERP address" per customer of type "ERP customer". |
| Phone number | CRM will restrict phone numbers so that there can only be two phone numbers per customer or contact. |
| E-mail address | CRM will restrict e-mail addresses so that there can only be one e-mail address per customer or contact. |

**Make a note**

Note that there are a number of rules that need to be built into the CRM UI business logic to ensure that the synchronization works successfully.

# Workshop

In our example, when we were defining rules for entity mapping we assumed there was a customer type field, a contact type field, and so on. What alternatives are there? (Hint: use the default contact or first created contact and add new field check box.) Which option is the best fit for your CRM application?

For the contact entity mapping we had three rules. Are all three rules necessary? What is the effect of not implementing some of the rules (hint: worse user experience, the chance of some incoherent data over time, but quicker to implement).

For the e-mail and phone number entity mapping we defined a rule that CRM would be customized to only have two phone numbers and one e-mail address per customer or contact, so that it could match the ERP rules. What would you do if you could not limit the number of phone numbers and e-mail addresses in CRM? (Hint: consider using types, as are recommended for contacts and addresses.)

Design the entity mappings for customers for your CRM and ERP applications.

# Step 3 – defining the unique identifiers

Now that we have defined the entities and the rules for how they will map to each other, we need to define how we will uniquely identify every record that we are synchronizing.

An example can explain why we need to do this. Let's say that we have customer information that is stored in both CRM and ERP, and that we are synchronizing the customer information between the two applications:

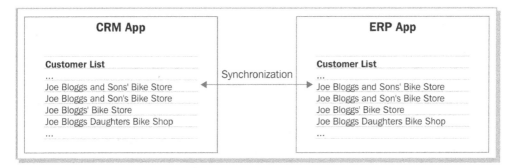

When the data changes in the ERP side, we need to synchronize the data with CRM and update the ERP side. One of the customer names is "Joe Bloggs and Sons' Bike Store".

If Joe Bloggs changes the name of his company to "Joe Bloggs and Daughters' Bike Store", and the change is made in the ERP we need to synchronize the change to the CRM. But how do we know which record to change in CRM? There are lots of records with similar names. There even is a customer that is already called "Joe Bloggs Daughters Bike Shop", but that is the wrong record to change.

Clearly, we need an unambiguous way to uniquely identify the correct record to change.

In fact, this is a challenge for all data that we are synchronizing between ERP and CRM, whether it is customer, contact, address, phone number, or e-mail address information.

# Strategies for uniquely identifying records

There are several techniques for uniquely identifying records, which we will discuss:

> ➤ Use a unique identifier such as database ID or reference number
> ➤ Use a parent/child relationship

# Using a unique identifier such as database IDs or reference numbers

Sometimes, software applications use unique identifiers in their data records. These are ideal for use as unique identifiers because they cannot be changed. Database unique identifiers are rarely available, and the method that is used most frequently is to use the customer reference number as the unique identifier:

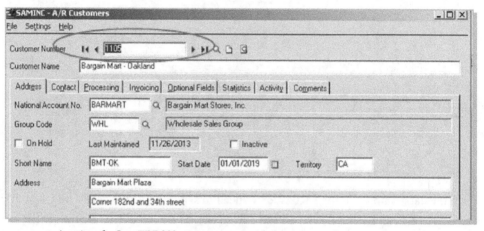

*A section of a Sage ERP 300 customer screen, with the customer reference number circled*

Customer reference numbers are visible to the user, which is okay. Unfortunately, in many ERP applications they are also editable by the user. If they are editable by the user this means they can change, and this makes them less satisfactory as unique identifiers. However, let's assume for the time being that we can use them.

If we are using the ERP customer reference number we need to copy the ERP customer reference number to the CRM customers that we are synchronizing:

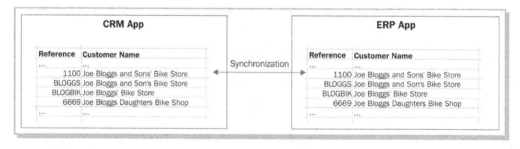

Once we have done that we can use the customer references to identify the customer.

For example, in a scenario where Joe Bloggs changed his company name from "Joe Bloggs and Sons' Bike Store" to "Joe Bloggs and Daughters' Bike Store", we could use the customer reference 1100 to identify the correct record.

A strategy is needed to consider the fact that the customer reference can be changed in the ERP application. There are no ideal solutions, but some options that can be considered are:

➤ Turn off the option to change customer references in the ERP, or document that this is not supported.

➤ Implement a customization so that whenever a customer reference changes in ERP it will trigger some customized code to make the update in CRM. The code will need to know the old reference and the new reference so that it will know what to update.

## Use a parent/child relationship of the entities

This method can be used for entities that have a parent relationship with another entity. The entity diagram can be used to identify which entities are parents of other entities:

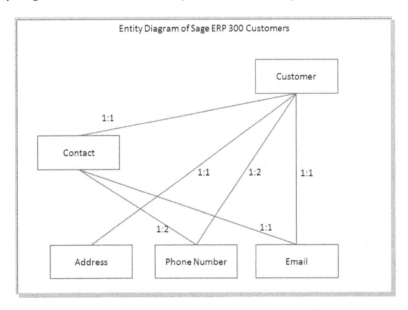

You can use the entity diagrams to define parent / child relationships. The entity below another entity is a child of that entity

In our entity diagram for customers, we can see that a contact is a child of a customer, and an address, phone number, and e-mail address is a child of a contact or a customer.

What this means is that a contact is always associated with a customer, and an address, phone number or e-mail address is always associated with a contact or customer:

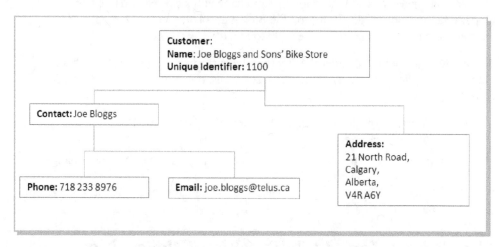

The preceding figure is an example of "Joe Bloggs and Sons' Bike Store" with other information that may be synchronized. We can synch the other information as child information of "Joe Bloggs and Sons' Bike Store", using the customer's unique identifier.

For example, if we are synchronizing the customer "Joe Bloggs and Sons' Bike Store" we will have other information such as contact information and address, phone, and e-mail information. This information is associated with the customer "Joe Bloggs and Sons' Bike Store", it does not exist separately from the customer. This means that we can reuse the unique identifier for the customer "Joe Bloggs and Sons' Bike Store", to identify the other information. In general, only the customer needs a unique identifier.

For example, the contact "Joe Bloggs" can be partially identified by looking for contacts associated with the customer with unique identifier 1100. We need one more piece of information. In our CRM example a customer can have many contacts, so this will not uniquely identify "Joe Bloggs". In the previous section on entity mapping we created a rule that contacts that are synchronized would have a contact type "ERP contact". There can only be one contact of type "ERP contact" per customer. If we look for contacts of type "ERP contact" that are associated with customer identifier 1100, we will uniquely identify the contact "Joe Bloggs".

We can use a similar exercise to uniquely identify the other information, such as address, phone number, and e-mails.

# Summary of unique identifiers

In our worked example, let's say that the unique identifiers for the entities will be as follows:

| Entity | Unique identifier |
|---|---|
| Customer | Customer reference number—this needs to be copied from the ERP to CRM for every customer that is synchronized. |
| Contact | Use a parent / child relationship between contact and customer. The contact will be the only contact of type "ERP Contact" associated with the customer's reference number. |
| Address | Use a parent / child relationship between address and customer. The address will be the only address of type "ERP Address " associated with the customer's reference number. |
| Phone number | This is an exercise; see the workshop. |
| E-mail address | Use a parent / child relationship between e-mail address and customer or contact. The e-mail address will be the only e-mail address associated with the customer, or the contact. |

Note that the only item that needs a unique reference is the customer. The other records can be deduced from their relationship with the customer. This is a realistic scenario as ERP applications in many cases do not have in-built unique identifiers for every piece of data.

# Workshop

In this section we used the parent child relationships combined with the "types" of the record in CRM to uniquely identify child records such as contact, address, phone number, and e-mail address. In our worked example this technique would not work for the phone numbers. Why? (Hint: we have two phone numbers for a contact, but they are not differentiated from each other—how can this be? The recommended answer is in the summary of backend design section.)

In this section we talk about using ERP data for the unique identifier, such as the ERP database ID, or the ERP customer reference. Why do we not consider using CRM identifiers? (Hint: it is easier to customized CRM, so it is easier to put ERP identifiers into CRM than to put CRM identifiers into ERP).

Define the unique identifiers for customers in your CRM to ERP integration. Define the unique identifiers for all child records that will be synchronized.

# Step 4 – defining the fields and field mappings

We have defined the entities, how they relate to each other, and how they will be uniquely identified. The next step is to identify, for each entity, which fields we will be synchronizing and how they will map to each other. We also need to gather field characteristics such as type and size.

## Customer field mapping

We shall start by looking at the customer entity. We make a list of the customer fields in the ERP that we would like to synchronize with CRM:

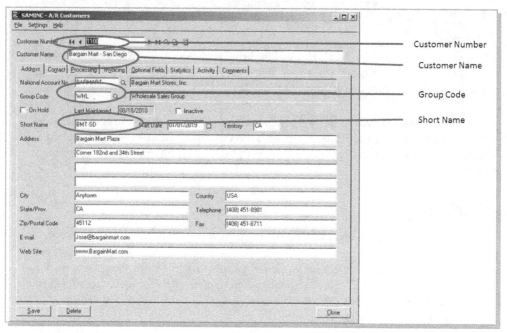

*Sage ERP 300 customer screen showing some fields for the customer entity that we would like to synchronize*

We can make the list by looking at the ERP UI and picking out what fields we would like to synchronize. The previous screenshot shows a Sage ERP 300 customer screen with some useful fields circled. A full list of ERP customer fields that would be useful to synch is, for example:

| ERP customer fields |
|---|
| Customer number |
| Customer name |
| Group code |

| |
|---|
| Short name |
| Terms code |
| Tax group |
| Credit limit |
| Credit on hold status |
| Active/inactive status |

The next thing we need to do is look at the type of the field. Fields in applications have different types. Some common field types that we will use are:

➤ **String**: A string is a sequence of characters. Examples of a string are company name, address line, and contact name. Strings have a maximum length. For example a company name might have a max length of 60 characters. The short name might have a max length of 10 characters.

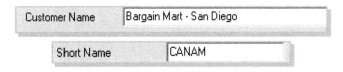

➤ **Selection**: A selection is a type of field where the user is given a selection of pre-canned strings to choose from. For example a user can select a country from a list of country names:

➤ **Number**: A number is a field that is a whole number such as 10 or 300. An example might be the number of days to pay an invoice:

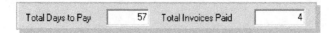

➤ **Decimal**: A decimal is a field that is a number which can have decimal places. This can be used to show currency amounts such as credit limits:

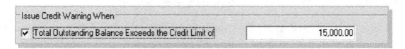

➤ **Percentage**: A percentage is a field that is a percentage value. For example a discount percentage might be 10 percent:

➤ **Date**: A date field is a field that shows a date. For example the opened data of an order, or the due date of an invoice, would be a date such as September, 20 2015:

➤ **Checkbox**: A checkbox is a field with only two values, checked or not checked. For example the credit on hold status of a customer is either on hold or not on hold:

When we are synchronizing fields we need to make sure that fields of the similar type are synchronized with each other.

We also need to identify the corresponding customer fields in CRM. For each field in our table, we need to identify whether a field for it exists in CRM. If the field exists, we need to make sure that the field types match, and if it is a string type, we need to check the max length of the string.

For this exercise, we will use the CRM customer fields in a standalone edition of SageCRM. We will update the table that we have created:

| ERP customer fields | ERP field type | CRM customer field | CRM customer field type |
|---|---|---|---|
| Customer number | String (length 12)<br><br>Note: this is a special field as it is our unique identifier | - | |
| Customer name | String (length 60) | Company name | String (length 50) |
| Group code | String (length 6) | - | |
| Short name | String (length 10) | - | |
| Terms code | String (length 6) | - | |
| Tax group | String (length 6) | - | |
| Credit limit | Decimal | - | |
| Credit on hold status | Checkbox | - | |
| Active/ inactive status | Checkbox | - | |
| - | - | Type | String<br><br>Note that this must be set to type = "ERP Customer" |

The table now shows the list of ERP customer fields with types that will be synchronized with CRM if they map to a CRM field. For completeness the CRM field called "Type" has been added because we created a rule in the entity mapping section that all customers that are synchronized should have the type = "ERP Customer".

We can see from the table that most of the ERP customer fields that we wish to synchronize to CRM do not exist in the CRM application.

As part of the integration we will need to add the missing fields making sure they are of the same type as the ERP fields. If they are strings we must make sure they are the same length as their corresponding ERP fields.

If mapped string fields are of a different length, such as the customer name, it can lead to data being truncated (cut off) when it is synchronized. If possible, it is recommended to lengthen the CRM customer name field so that it matches the length of the ERP customer name field.

We now need to do the same exercise for the other entities: contact, address, phone number, and e-mail address. We will not go through the detailed steps for these entities, but we will show you what the end result is and discuss any anomalies.

# Contact field mappings

For our exercise, here is what the contact field mappings table looks like:

| ERP contact fields | ERP field type | CRM contact field | CRM field type |
|---|---|---|---|
| Contact name | String (length 60) | First name | String (60) |
| | | Last name | String (60) |
| - | - | - | Customer reference<br><br>Note that this is a special field to link the contact with the customer reference |
| - | - | Type | String<br><br>Note that this must be set to type = "ERP Contact" |

In our exercise the fields of a contact to synchronize are just the contact name. In our ERP example the contact name is one field, but the contact name is split into two fields in CRM. There is a first name and a last name in CRM.

This is our first example of the fields in ERP being different to their corresponding fields in CRM. Sometimes when this situation occurs there is no ideal solution and a compromise needs to be found, which is to make the best of different options.

One approach to resolve issues like this is to try to customize CRM so that it is more like ERP. In this example we may try to remove the first name field from CRM so that it only has one name field, and we are only synchronizing the names to the last name. This may be more difficult than it seems if the CRM application makes a lot of use of the field that you wish to remove.

Alternatively the data can be transformed during the synchronization so that it fits the appropriate fields. In this example we could try splitting the contact name into the first and last name when bringing it from ERP to CRM. When the data is going the other way we could try joining the first and last name when bringing the contact name from CRM to ERP. This works some of the time, but the concern is that it is very difficult to design software to reliably pick out the first name of a string.

The other interesting part of the contact field mapping table is the customer reference field. In our discussion on unique identifiers we decided that for our example the contact will be uniquely identified by being associated with a customer, and having the type "ERP contact". The customer reference field is where the reference to the customer is stored. This field will already exist in the CRM application, and it needs to be filled in correctly by the synchronization software.

# Address field mappings

The address field mappings are contained in the following table:

| ERP address fields | ERP field type | CRM address fields | CRM field type |
|---|---|---|---|
| Address 1 | String (length 60) | Address 1 | String (length 30) |
| Address 2 | String (length 60) | Address 2 | String (length 30) |
| Address 3 | String (length 60) | Address 3 | String (length 30) |
| Address 4 | String (length 60) | Address 4 | String (length 30) |
| City | String (length 30) | City | String (length 30) |
| State | String (length 30) | State | String (length 30) |
| Country | String (length 30) | Country | Selection |
| Zip code | String (length 20) | Zip code | String (length 10) |
| - | - | - | Customer reference<br><br>Note that this is a special field to link the address with the customer reference |
| - | - | Type | String<br><br>Note that this must be set to type = "ERP Address" |

The table shows how the ERP address fields map to the CRM fields. The fields in the ERP address entity that are to be synchronized map very well with the fields in the CRM application, for our example, but there are some differences to note.

The first difference is that the lengths of the strings are different for some of the address fields. It is recommended to change the string lengths so that they match.

Secondly, the country field in ERP is a string, while the country field in CRM is a selection list. This needs to be dealt with by the synchronization code. For example you could enter the country of United States of America into the address in ERP, or America, or USA. They all mean the same thing. The synchronization code needs to know that all three of this different ways of entering United States of America all map to the one country name.

Finally note that the address also has to have a reference to the customer or contact that it is a child of, and the type of the address needs to be set to "ERP Address".

# Phone number field mappings

The phone number field mappings are contained in the following table:

| ERP phone fields | ERP field type | CRM phone fields | CRM field type |
|---|---|---|---|
| Phone number | String (length 30) | Area code | String (length 4) |
| | | Phone Number | String (length 30) |
| - | - | - | Customer reference<br><br>Note that this is a special field to link the phone number with the customer or contact reference |

The table shows how the ERP phone fields map to the CRM fields. In this example, the phone number in ERP maps to two fields in CRM, the area code and the phone number. There are two ways of tackling this issue. The first way is to try to make CRM be more like the ERP, in this case by removing the area code from CRM, so that there is only one field for phone number in both CRM and ERP. This may or may not be possible.

The second way is by getting the synchronization code to split the phone number into an area code and phone number when the phone number comes from ERP, and to join the area code and phone number into one number when the phone number comes from CRM. If this second option is used, note also that the string lengths in CRM total to 34 for the phone number plus area code, and they are only 30 for the ERP phone number, so there is a possibility of truncation of data.

# E-mail field mappings

The e-mail field mappings are contained in the following table:

| ERP e-mail fields | ERP field type | CRM e-mail fields | CRM field type |
|---|---|---|---|
| E-mail address | String (length 60) | E-mail address | String (length 50) |
| - | - | - | Customer reference<br><br>Note that this is a special field to link the e-mail address with the customer or contact reference |

The table shows how the ERP e-mail address field maps to the CRM field. In this example, the length of the e-mail address is longer in the ERP than in the CRM. If possible the string lengths should be made the same to avoid truncation of data.

## Workshop

Create field mappings tables for customer, contact, address, phone number, and e-mail address for your CRM to ERP integration.

# Step 5 – defining the CRUD rules

We have defined the entities, how they relate to each other, how they will be uniquely identified, and we have defined the fields for each entity and how they map between CRM and ERP fields.

We now need to define the CRUD rules for our synchronization. **CRUD** is an acronym for "**Create, Read, Update, and Delete**". It describes the four main operations that you can carry out on a data record. Customer information can be created, read, updated, and deleted on both the CRM and the ERP application. Now that we are synchronizing data, a CRUD action on the CRM side could have an impact on the synchronization code, and, more importantly could have an eventual impact on the ERP application, and vice versa.

Read actions will have no impact on the synchronization. We need to examine each of the other CRUD actions; Create, Update, and Delete, on both the CRM side and the ERP side, and decide how they will affect the synchronization design and the other application. We start by looking at the create operations on both CRM and ERP sides.

# Synchronizing create actions on ERP and CRM

It is possible for users to create customers in both the CRM and the ERP application:

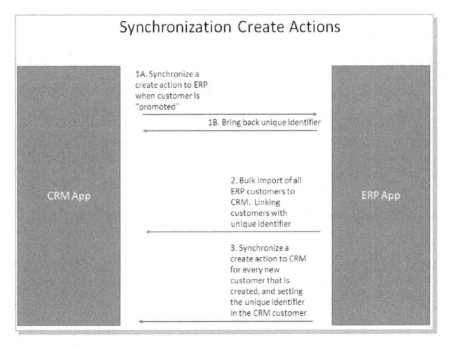

In our use cases discussion, we stated that new customers should be synchronized in the following scenarios:

> ➤ Importing ERP customers to CRM in bulk
> ➤ Newly created ERP customers should be synchronized to CRM
> ➤ Qualified CRM customers should be "promoted" to ERP

# Importing ERP customers to CRM in bulk

In the use cases for our example, there are several thousand ERP customers that are not in CRMthat need to be copied over. Also, it is good practice to have a "bulk import" option in the integration that will copy over all ERP customers, as a way of occasionally making sure that all the ERP customer information matches the CRM customer information.

The bulk import option can be triggered from a new button in the administration area of the CRM UI. Behind the scenes this should raise a flag for the synchronization software to copy all ERP customers from ERP to CRM.

If we are using a hub and spoke method of synchronization the bulk import request would trigger a synchronization. In a normal synchronization cycle, the broker checks the ERP for customers that have changed since the last synchronization cycle. In a bulk import the broker skips the step of checking what customers have changed, and would instead assume that all customers need to be re-imported. Customers that already exist in CRM, and were linked to ERP would be updated, and customers that only existed in ERP would be newly created in CRM.

If we are using a point to point method of synchronization, the bulk import request would need to call bespoke synchronization code that is written to read all the ERP customers and write them to the CRM database. As with the hub and spoke method, customers that already exist in CRM and are linked with ERP customers would be updated, and customers that only existed in ERP would be newly created in CRM.

# Newly created ERP customers should be synchronized to CRM

Newly created customers in ERP should be automatically synchronized to CRM. The unique identifier for the customer should be brought over with the synchronization so they are linked together correctly.

# Qualified CRM customers should be "promoted" to ERP

It should be possible to promote CRM customers to ERP. This is different to the ERP case because not all CRM customers are synchronized to ERP. The action of selecting a customer to be copied over to ERP is user initiated and is called "promotion".

There are several points of discussion on the promotion of a customer feature:

> ➤ It is manually triggered by a user

> ➤ The conditions for adding a customer to ERP must be considered

> ➤ The unique identifier for a promoted customer must be set

> ➤ There must be a way to tell whether a CRM customer has been successfully "promoted"

# Manual triggering of a customer promotion

When a customer is promoted to ERP, it is newly created in ERP even though it has already existed in CRM for a while:

A button or other mechanism needs to be provided to the user to allow them to promote a customer from CRM to ERP. The previous screenshot shows an example "Promote to Customer" button in the SageCRM integration with Sage ERP 300.

# Conditions for adding a promoted customer to ERP

When a customer is "promoted" from CRM to ERP care needs to be taken to ensure that the customer has all the information necessary to be a full ERP accounts receivable customer. For example, you need to decide whether you want your sales users to be able to "promote" customers to ERP and then sell to them without having the new customer approved by a more senior member on the team, or by an ERP back office user. One approach when "promoting" customers to ERP is to create the customer in ERP with the status of "inactive" or on customer "credit hold". This means that somebody has to manually check the customer in ERP before any serious business can be done with them.

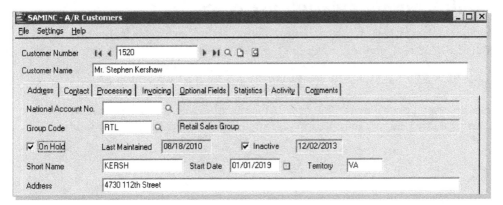

The preceding screenshot partially shows an accounts receivable customer in Sage 300, with the status of "inactive" and with the credit status "on hold". Customers promoted to the ERP can be created with these statii, to ensure that they are reviewed before sales business is done with them.

Alternatively, the "promotion" of a customer workflow in CRM can include steps to ensure that adequate data is entered for the customer before it is promoted to ERP, perhaps by adding mandatory fields for back office data such as tax group, terms code, credit limit, and/or by making sure that only appropriate users have access to approve the "promotion". (See the workshop for more on this option.)

## Setting the unique identifier for a promoted customer

Setting the unique identifier in the case of promoted CRM customers being synchronized to ERP is more complicated. In the section on unique identifiers, we discussed that the unique identifier for a customer is either the ERP database unique reference or the ERP customer reference. When the customer is in CRM and not in ERP, there is no unique identifier because the record is not in ERP yet. When the synchronization code creates the new customer in ERP, it needs to take the unique identifier and copy it back to the CRM customer, and update the CRM customer with the unique identifier so that the customer is correctly linked between CRM and ERP.

## Discovering whether a CRM customer has been successfully "promoted"

A promoted customer in CRM is different to a non-promoted customer in CRM because it is linked to an ERP customer counterpart. It is important to be able to tell from looking at a customer whether they have been successfully "promoted" to ERP. One way to do this is to update the CRM customer type to "ERP customer" only when it is successfully promoted. Another way is to add a checkbox to the customer schema called "promoted" and check the checkbox when it is successfully promoted. It is also useful to add a date/timestamp to the customer record that is set when a customer promotion occurs.

For our exercise we will add the rule that we will update the CRM customer type to "ERP customer" when the customer is successfully promoted.

## Limiting other creation use cases

We have only considered up to now the creation of customers. What about the creation of contacts, addresses, phone numbers, or e-mail addresses? When a new customer is created in many cases a new contact, address, and other contact information are added at the same time.

It is, however, possible in an ERP or CRM application to create a customer with no address or other contact information at first, and then to add the information later.

This leads to many new synchronization use cases. For example the following creation use cases, or a combination of the following use cases, would need to be supported from ERP to CRM or from CRM to ERP:

- ➤ Adding a new contact to an existing customer
- ➤ Adding a new address to an existing customer
- ➤ Adding a new phone number to an existing customer
- ➤ Adding a new e-mail address to an existing customer
- ➤ Adding a new phone number to an existing contact
- ➤ Adding a new e-mail address to an existing contact

There is a strategy that can be used to eliminate the need to support these additional use cases and save on development effort.

In the CRM to ERP direction, the way to eliminate these additional use cases is to only allow the promotion of a customer if all the contact, address, phone, and e-mail information have already been added to the customer. This eliminates the need to support any of the user cases in the previous list.

In the ERP to CRM direction, when synchronizing a new customer from ERP to CRM, the synchronization code should always create all the child records: contact, address, phone, and e-mail address information. Even if there is some information missing, for example if there is no e-mail address, create the e-mail address and leave the e-mail address blank.

In the future, when an e-mail address is added to the customer on the ERP side, the synchronization can treat it as an update, and update the blank e-mail address on the CRM side. All the update use cases need to be supported anyway, so it is no additional work.

## Summary of synch creation use cases

The table shows the summary of creation use cases:

| Entity | Synching creates from ERP to CRM? | Synching creates from CRM to ERP? |
|---|---|---|
| Customer | Yes, including the bulk import option | Yes, as the promotion of a customer |
| Contact | No | No |
| Address | No | No |
| Phone number | No | No |
| E-mail address | No | No |

*Summary of which entities are created in CRM and ERP*

Child entities, such as contacts, addresses, phone numbers, and e-mail addresses are created as part of the initial creation of a customer, and are not treated separately. We can focus on customer creation, provided that the creation of child entities is included in the customer creation and is not treated separately.

# Synchronizing update actions on CRM and ERP

It is possible to update customer information in both CRM and ERP. In our use cases we support the synchronization of updates in both directions, from ERP to CRM and from CRM to ERP.

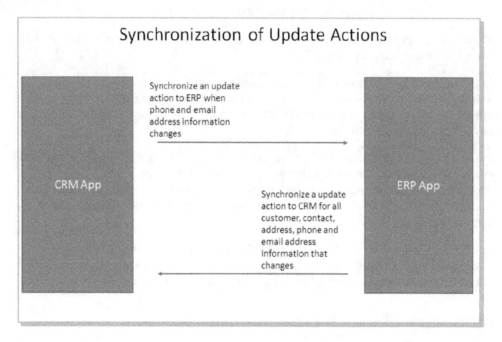

All customer information in ERP can be updated and synchronized to CRM. Limited customer information in CRM can be updated and synchronized to ERP.

When a user updates customer information on the ERP side the synchronization code should pick up the change and send it over to the CRM as an update action on the CRM customer. This should take place for changes to any customer information including any child information such as contact, address, phone number, or e-mail address.

On the CRM side a decision needs to be made on what parts of a customer are allowed to be changed. In Chapter 2 that we would like to allow users in CRM to be able to change e-mail addresses and phone number information for a customer in CRM. We further discussed how we should not allow a user in CRM to be able to change a customer's credit limit, or credit on hold status in CRM, as that data should only be set in the ERP. There are also areas that are up for discussion such as a customer's name or a customer's address.

For the sake of our worked example, we shall decide that the only information on a CRM customer that can be edited will be the phone numbers and e-mail addresses. This means that in the CRM UI we need to create a new rule to ensure that the other customer information is read only in CRM.

## Summary of synch update use cases

This table shows a summary of update use cases:

| Entity | Synch of updates from ERP to CRM? | Synch of updates from CRM to ERP? |
|---|---|---|
| Customer | Yes | No* |
| Contact | Yes | No* |
| Address | Yes | No* |
| Phone Number | Yes | Yes |
| E-mail address | Yes | Yes |

Note that the read only status of customers, contacts, and addresses in CRM needs to be enforced by a UI customization in CRM.

The table shows a summary of which entities are updateable in CRM and ERP. Three entities will not be updateable in CRM. This will need to be enforced in the CRM UI by a customization.

## Synchronizing delete actions on CRM and ERP

The use cases for our sample company do not mention the deletion of information, but we know that it is possible for customers to be deleted from ERP and CRM, and so we need to plan how to deal with that in the synchronization.

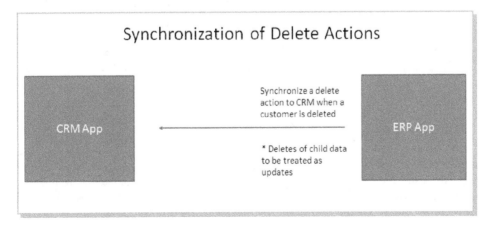

Customer information in ERP can be deleted and this can be synchronized to CRM. Customers in CRM will be set to be not deletable if they are linked with an ERP customer.

On the ERP side, it is possible for users to delete customers, though it is more common to make the customer inactive. The synchronization code should detect whether customers on ERP have been deleted and bring the change to CRM, deleting the customer in CRM. The deletion of a customer should include the deletion of all the child entities, contact, address, phone number, and e-mail address.

On the ERP side it may be possible to delete the 'child' entities while leaving the customer undeleted. For example, it may be possible to delete a customer address, while leaving the customer still in ERP. In order to reduce the number of delete use cases that need to be supported it is recommended to treat the deletion of a child entity as an update, which blanks out the information, instead of a delete.

For example if a customer's address is deleted in ERP, the synchronization code should treat it as an update, by updating the customer in CRM, and blanking out the address information. All the update use cases need to be supported anyway, so it is no additional work.

On the CRM side, in general it is possible to delete customers. However you need to decide whether it is a good idea to allow a user in CRM to delete a customer that is linked with an ERP customer. The linked customer in ERP may have open invoices and other useful information. It is recommended to not allow the deletion of a CRM customer, in the case that it is linked with an ERP customer. This will need to be implemented in a UI customization. Similarly it is recommended to not allow the deletion of a customer's child data, if it is linked with the ERP application. (Refer to the question in the workshop.)

# Summary of synch delete use cases

This table shows a summary of delete use cases:

| Entity | Synch of deletes from ERP to CRM? | Synch of deletes from CRM to ERP? |
|---|---|---|
| Customer | Yes | No |
| Contact | No | No |
| Address | No | No |
| Phone Number | No | No |
| E-mail address | No | No |

The previous table shows a summary of which entities can be deleted in CRM and ERP. When customers are deleted in ERP all their child data should be deleted as well. It should not be possible to delete CRM customers that are linked with the ERP because the customer may have valuable information in the ERP. Instead, the safe option is for the user to delete the customer in ERP and this will be synchronized to CRM.

# Workshop

Define, create, update, and delete synchronization rules for customers, contacts, addresses, phone numbers, and e-mail addresses for your CRM to ERP integration.

# Security

We have defined the entities, how they relate to each other, how they will be uniquely identified, and we have defined the fields for each entity and how they map between CRM and ERP fields, and the CRUD synchronization actions.

We now need to review the security rules for the contact integration. The integration will change the data that is available in the CRM application and will change the actions that users can do, including having the ability to indirectly change ERP data.

The flexibility that you will have in implementing security rules depends on your CRM application.

A good way to review the security is to look at each of the CRUD actions in turn (create, read, update and delete), starting with the read action.

## Security for "read" information

The new information that can be read in CRM is all the ERP accounts receivable customers, including some ERP-specific information such as tax group, payment terms, and credit on hold status, their contacts, addresses, phone numbers, and e-mail addresses. By default, any user who can look at customers in the CRM application will be able to see this information. If your CRM application has a data export feature, any users with access to this feature will be able to do a data export of all your accounts receivable customers.

Some approaches include one, or a combination of some, of the following:

> **No restriction**: You could decide that you are comfortable with all your users being able to view your ERP customer information.

> **Restricting the data export option**: You should at least review who has access to your data export feature in CRM, if there is one.

> **Restricting the customer list**: CRM customers that are linked with ERP will have the customer type "ERP customer", and they are therefore easy to distinguish between the other CRM customers that are in CRM only. You could decide that you only want a subset of users to be able to see your CRM customers with type "ERP customer", or perhaps the members of certain teams, or users who perform a certain role.

> **Restricting some of the customer information**: You could decide that you are comfortable with the users seeing some of the customer information, but that maybe they should not be able to see the ERP-specific information such as the credit limit or payment terms. You will need to hide those fields for certain users as a UI customization.

# Security for create, update, and delete information

Customers can be created in CRM and synchronized to ERP as new customers. Customer information, such as e-mail address and phone number, can be updated in CRM and synchronized to the ERP.

The approach to security for the creation of customers should be one of the following options:

> **No restriction**: You could decide that you are comfortable with all users who can view customers in CRM being able to promote any CRM customer to the ERP.

> **Restrict access to the promote button**: You could decide that only a subset of users, or a certain team, or users with a certain role, should be allowed to promote customers to ERP. Hide the promote button from users who should not be allowed to promote customers.

> **Restrict update access**: You could decide that only a subset of users, or a certain team, or users with a certain role, should be allowed to update customer e-mail address and phone number information and have that information synchronized to ERP.

In our use case, once a CRM customer is promoted to ERP, it will not be possible to delete it and so there are no delete actions to be concerned about.

## Security summary

A summary of security areas is in the following table:

| Action in CRM | Recommendation |
| --- | --- |
| Read | Review users with read access, and change permissions as necessary |
| Create | Review users with create access, and hide promote button as necessary |
| Update | Review users with update access, and change permissions on updateable fields as necessary |
| Delete | No action needed |

In general, the use cases that now affect CRM and ERP data should be reviewed, and access permissions should be modified as necessary.

## Workshop

Decide which CRM users should be allowed to view ERP customer information in CRM. Should it be per user, per team, or per user role? How will this be enforced in your CRM?

Decide which CRM users should be allowed to promote customers from CRM to ERP. Should it be per user, per team, or per user role? How will this be enforced in your CRM?

Decide which CRM users should be to update CRM customer information that is synchronized to ERP. Should it be per user, per team, or per user role? How will this be enforced in your CRM?

We have not discussed security on the ERP side when changes to ERP customers affect CRM customers. When ERP customers are created, updated, or deleted in ERP the changes will be synchronized to CRM customers. By default, all users with edit rights on ERP customers will be able to make changes. Do a review of which users on the ERP application will be able to make changes to ERP customer information.

# CRM UI changes

We have defined the entities, how they relate to each other, how they will be uniquely identified, and we have defined the fields for each entity and how they map between CRM and ERP fields, the CRUD synchronization actions, and we have considered the security implications for the changes we will be making.

We will now identify the UI changes to CRM that will need to be made for each entity.

## UI changes to customer screens

New fields are being added to the customer entity that will need to be shown on the customer screen:

- ➤ Customer number
- ➤ Group code
- ➤ Short name
- ➤ Terms code
- ➤ Credit limit
- ➤ Credit on hold status
- ➤ Active/inactive status

A field on the customer screen that will change is:

- ➤ Type: There will a new type that can be shown for a customer "ERP customer"

A new UI rule that will be added is:

- ➤ When a customer is of type "ERP customer" it should not be editable or deletable. This is because we are not synchronizing updates or deletes of customers from CRM to ERP.

A new UI button that will be added is:

> ➤ **Promote Button**: The promote button will mark that a customer should be "promoted" to ERP. The code will need to make a change that will signify that the customer is ready for synch, for example, by updating a field in the schema for the customer record.

# UI changes to contact screens

A field on the contact screen that will change is:

> ➤ **Type**: There will a new type that can be shown for a contact: "ERP contact"

A new UI rule that will be added is:

> ➤ When a contact is of type "ERP contact" it should not be editable or deletable. This is because we are not synchronizing updates or deletes of contacts from CRM to ERP.

# UI changes to address screens

A field on the address screen that will change is:

> ➤ Type: There will a new type that can be shown for a contact: "ERP address"

A new UI rule that will be added is:

> ➤ When an address is of type "ERP address" it should not be editable or deletable. This is because we are not synchronizing updates or deletes of addresses from CRM to ERP. UI changes to phone screens.

As we discussed in our use cases, the number of phone numbers in CRM will be restricted so that there can only be two phone numbers per customer or contact.

# UI changes to e-mail address screens

As we discussed in our use cases, the number of e-mail addresses in CRM will be restricted so that there can only be one e-mail address per customer or contact.

# Administration screen

A new administration screen needs to be added, which has a button that starts a full import of all ERP customers.

# Reports/dashboard changes

The additional customer information that will be brought to CRM from ERP can be added to existing reports and/or dashboards, or new reports and/or dashboards can be created for them. Some examples of new reports or dashboards that be created are:

- ➤ A list of customers in ERP that are currently inactive or active
- ➤ A list of customers in ERP that are currently on credit hold
- ➤ A list of customers sorted by credit limit

# Workshop

Gather together all the design work that you have completed for this chapter so far, and use the information to compile a list of UI changes that will need to be made.

Define which reports and/or dashboards should be updated or created to make use of the new data that is available in CRM.

# Summary

In this chapter, we designed a contact management integration.

We started off by describing a real-world scenario for a fictional business called RideRight Bike Parts Company, which has a need for a contact management integration.

We identified the uses cases, and reframed them as CRM workflows that we needed to implement:

- ➤ The ability to promote a CRM customer to ERP
- ➤ Automatic synch of ERP customers from ERP to CRM, both as a bulk import and for incremental creates and updates
- ➤ Ability to view ERP customer information on CRM customer screens

We then designed the integration solution using the real-world applications of SageCRM and Sage ERP 300, to provide some context. The design of the integration is in several steps:

1. Create entity diagrams
2. Map the entity diagrams
3. Define the unique identifiers
4. Define the fields and field mappings
5. Define the CRUD rules

As this is the first time we designed an integration we spent some time explaining the steps as we worked through examples for our workflows. In the workshops, you were asked to follow along using your CRM and ERP applications.

We discussed the security implications of the changes we are making. It is important to review and control which users have access to the new ERP data that will appear in CRM.

Finally, we summarized the UI customizations that will be required for the contact integration workflows. At this point the design is completed for the contact management integration. The next step is to develop the solution. The chapter called "How to develop and maintain an integration" discusses the next development stage in more detail.

In the next chapter we design the sales management integration. The sales management integration builds on the contact management integration. It is an integration for sales users.

# 4

# How to Build a Sales Management Integration

The previous chapter covered the design of a contact management integration. In this chapter, we will build on this by adding a sales management integration for sales users.

We will use real-world scenarios for our fictional company, RideRight Bike Parts Company, to build up the use cases. We will then design CRM-integrated workflows for those use cases.

In the workshop at the end of the chapter, we will go over some additional advanced use cases.

## Sales management integration use cases

RideRight Bike Parts Company have implemented a contact management integration between their CRM and ERP applications, and their CRM users are very happy with the improvements as they can now access customer information that is shared between the CRM and ERP applications. They see the benefits of not having to enter data twice, and being able to see more complete and accurate customer information on their CRM screens. Now they are asking for more.

The sales team has identified disconnects in the sales management workflows that they would like fixed, and which will bring further improvements in productivity:

1. The RideRight sales team sells to bike stores across Canada. Many of their customers are long-term customers who they have been dealing with for years. The RideRight sales team uses the CRM interactions feature for managing their communications with their customers, and the opportunities feature for managing sales opportunities. They find that they regularly have to leave the CRM application and go to the ERP application to complete their tasks. This happens most often when they use features that are only in the ERP, for example:

   ➤ When they need to create a quote for a customer
   ➤ When they need to take an order for a customer
   ➤ When they need to check on previous quotes or the order history for a customer

2. The RideRight sales team occasionally works outside the office. For example, they run promotions at bike-related trade shows across Canada, and sometimes make trips across the country to visit their top customers. When they go outside the office, they have access to their CRM application, but they do not have access to the ERP application, and so they are unable to create quotes and orders or look at a customer's quote and order history. This is very inconvenient for the sales users. Again, the sales users would like access to this functionality in CRM so that they can use it when they are working outside the office.

3. In order to improve productivity, the CRM sales team would like to be able to manage orders and quotes in their CRM application from any location, not just within the office.

We will now take these business use cases and convert them to integration workflows to be implemented.

# Integration workflows

As part of our process of designing a sales management integration, we take the business use cases that we identified in the last section and convert them to new integration workflows.

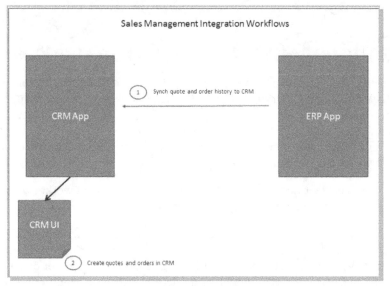

*New sales management integration workflows*

The preceding diagram shows the new integration workflows that we need to support in order to address the issues the sales team have identified. We will now explore them in more detail. They offer:

➤ The ability to create quotes and orders in CRM

➤ The ability to view quote and order history in CRM

# Ability to create quotes and orders

When CRM sales users wish to create a quote or an order for a customer, they need to leave their CRM application and open up their ERP application. This can be frustrating. With the new integration, the sales workflow can be changed in CRM so that the user will be able to click on a button to open up a quote or order entry screen and create a quote or order from within the CRM application. The quote or order will use all the business rules in ERP, including the correct price lists, tax amounts, and inventory confirmation, and it will be entered directly into the ERP application.

## How

Sales quote and sales order entry screens in ERP applications are very complex screens because there is so much business logic involved in creating a quote or order. The integration developer has the choice of re-implementing the screens in CRM and synchronizing the quotes and orders from CRM to ERP, or using the screen pop technology to pop an already existing ERP screen from the CRM application. For this worked example, we will use screen pops. Please check back to Chapter 2, How to Implement an Integration, for a reminder about what screen pops are, if needed.

# Ability to view quote and order history

When a CRM sales user wishes to view quote and order history, they need to leave their CRM application and open up their ERP application. The CRM application will be changed so that it will be possible to view quote and order history for a customer in the CRM application.

## How

The CRM implementer has the option of synchronizing the quote and order history from the ERP, or of viewing the quote and order history as a real-time view from the ERP. If the quote and order history information is synchronized, it has the benefit of being viewable in CRM dashboards and reports, and possibly by the marketing department to help with marketing campaigns. For this worked example, we will decide to synchronize the quote and order history information from ERP to CRM. This will be a one-way synchronization because the data is flowing from ERP to CRM only, and not back from CRM to ERP. The quotes and the orders that are synchronized will be read only in CRM.

## Design the integration

We have defined the workflows that need to be implemented. The next thing we need to do is to design the sales management integration. The design of the integration involves the same steps as for the contact management integration with one additional step, which is to design the screen pop feature for the new quotes and orders:

1. Create entity diagrams.
2. Map the entity diagrams.

3.  Define the unique Identifiers.

4.  Define the fields and field mappings.

5.  Define the CRUD rules.

6.  Design the screen pops.

The worked example will use the real-world applications of SageCRM and Sage ERP 300 so that it is realistic. The steps are likely to be very similar for your CRM and ERP application. In the workshops, you will be asked to do the corresponding design steps for your CRM and ERP applications.

# Step 1 – creating entity diagrams

The first step is to create entity diagrams of the data that we are synchronizing:

➤ Quotes

➤ Orders

As is common in many CRM applications, in our worked example, quotes and orders do not exist in SageCRM, and so we only need to do entity diagrams for how they appear in the ERP. If your CRM application has quotes and orders, you will need to do an entity diagram for the quotes and orders in CRM. They are very likely to be the same structure for both applications. Here's an example of how your entity diagram will look:

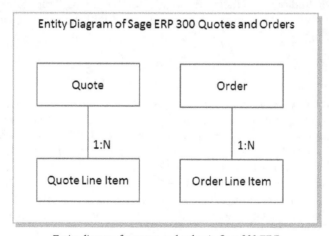

*Entity diagram for quotes and orders in Sage 300 ERP*

Quotes and orders each have line items. There is a line item for each item on a quote or order. The line item contains the item information, the quantity, and the cost. If we are doing a quote for two bicycle helmets and three bicycle front brakes, the quote will have two line items, one for the two bicycle helmets and one for the three front brakes, plus the costs of each line per item.

# Step 2 – mapping the entity diagrams to each other

The next step is to map the synchronized entities between ERP and CRM. The following table shows the rules that we will use for our worked example:

| Entity | Mapping Rule |
|---|---|
| Quote | Each quote in CRM will map to a quote in ERP. |
| Quote line item | Each quote line item in CRM will map to a quote line item in ERP. |
| Order | Each order in CRM will map to an order in ERP. |
| Order line item | Each order line item in CRM will map to an order line item in ERP. |

As quotes and orders and line items do not exist in CRM, we will simply create entities in CRM that will match the entities in ERP.

If your CRM has quote and order entities, you will need to map the ERP quote and order entities to the CRM quote and order entities that already exist. Your rules are likely to be very similar to the ones in the preceding table. By doing this, you will be able to synchronize the quotes and orders in the ERP into the CRM quotes and orders table, and they will be accessible for CRM users to view.

# Step 3 – defining the unique identifiers

Now that we have defined the entities and the rules for how they will map to each other, we need to define how we will uniquely identify every record that we are synchronizing. This will ensure that we synchronize one copy only of each quote and order for our RideRight CRM users to view.

The preferred method is to use the unique identifiers in the ERP database if they are available. If they are not available, use the quote or order reference number.

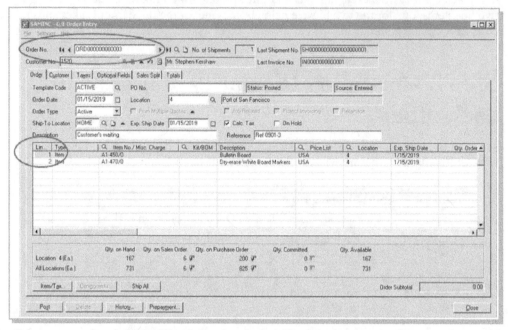

*Order entry screen from Sage ERP 300 with the order reference field circled, which is used as the unique reference, and the line number fields circled, which can be used to identify the line items*

For our worked example, we will use the quote or order reference number.

Orders and quotes are associated with customers, and each order and quote contains a customer number which links it to a customer. The customer number is a unique reference to a customer. We will use the customer number field on an order or quote to link it with a customer.

Orders and quotes are also associated with the salesperson who created them. We will synchronize the salesperson information to CRM so that it can be used to identify the CRM user who created the quote or order, if there is one.

The line items are children of the quote or order and they can be partially identified by their parent's reference number. There can be many line items for a quote or order, so they also need a unique number per line. In our worked example, we use the line number. Each line item can be uniquely referenced by a combination of its parent's reference number and the line number.

# Workshop

Create an entity relationship diagram for orders and quotes in your ERP.

If your CRM application has orders and quotes, do an entity relationship diagram for orders and quotes in your CMR, and do an entity mapping between orders and quotes in ERP and in CRM.

Define the unique references for orders and quotes and line items for your ERP, and if applicable, your CRM.

# Step 4 – defining the fields and field mappings

We have defined the entities, their mapping, and how they will be uniquely identified.

The next step is to identify, for each entity, which fields we will be synchronizing. We choose fields that will be used by our RideRight CRM users so that they will always have access to the quote and order information that they need.

We also need to gather field characteristics such as type and size. The fields do not exist in CRM, so we will do this exercise for the ERP fields, and then we will create identical fields in CRM to map to them.

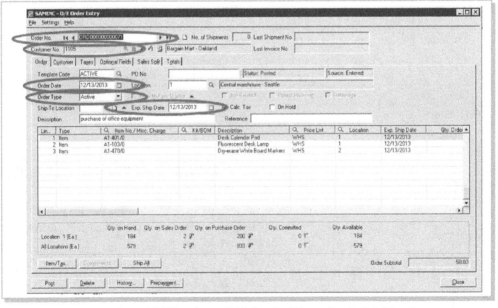

*The Order Entry screen in Sage ERP 100, with some fields that should be synchronized circled: order no, customer no, order date, order type, and expected ship date*

We start by looking at the UI in ERP and picking which fields we would like to bring to CRM. The preceding screenshot shows a Sage ERP 100 order entry screen, with some of the fields that we would like to synchronize circled. Note that the order number field will be the unique reference for the order. The customer number field will allow us to link the order with a customer.

In the following table, we will use a new type of field, called a **multi-line string**. A multi-line string is a string that has several lines in it, such as an address. For addresses that are associated with a contact, we brake the address lines into several fields, but for the quote and the order, we will treat the address as one field that is several lines long.

**Billing Address:**
Maverick Papers
220 Michigan Ave.
Chicago, IL 60601
United States of America

*Multi-line address field for a billing address in a SageCRM integration*

The quote and order fields that we would like to synchronize are shown in the following table:

| ERP order and quote fields | ERP field type |
|---|---|
| Document reference | String (12) |
| | Note that this is the unique reference for a quote or an order. |
| Customer number | String (12) |
| | Note that this is the unique reference to a customer. We use this field to associate an order or quote to a customer. |
| Description | String (60) |
| Document opened date | Date |
| Currency | String (5) |
| | This tells us which currency the quote or order is in, and is useful if we are dealing with a multi-currency system. |
| Salesperson | String (60) |
| | The name of the sales user. If this is the same name as a CRM user, the quote or order can be linked with a CRM user, which is useful for reporting. |
| Status | Selection (10) |
| | The selection values are active or inactive. |
| Expiration date | Date |
| | The date the quote expires. For quotes only. |

| ERP order and quote fields | ERP field type |
|---|---|
| Delivery date | Date<br><br>The date that the order is expected to be delivered. For orders only. |
| Purchase order reference | String (30)<br><br>A reference to the purchase order if one exists. For orders only. |
| Billing address | Multi-line string |
| Ship to address | Multi-line string |
| Shipping method | String (30)<br><br>How the order will be shipped, for example, flat rate, UPS blue rate, UPS 2nd day air, and so on. |
| Financial information | |
| Price sum | Decimal (the sum of all the line items' Quoted Price Sum values; see line item fields). |
| Discount type | Percentage or amount. |
| Discount percent | Number (if discount type is a percentage). |
| Discount amount | Decimal. |
| Freight amount | Decimal. |
| Sales tax amount | Decimal. |
| Deposit amount | Decimal. |
| Balance due | Decimal (sum of price sum, discount amount, freight amount, and sales tax amount minus Deposit Amount). |
| IsQuote | Boolean<br><br>This field only exists on the CRM side. If you are using one database table in CRM to store quotes and orders, this field can be used to tell which records are quotes and which are orders. Set the field to true if it is a quote, and set it to false if it is an order. |

In the bottom half of the table, there is a section with the subtitle **Financial information**. This list contains fields that summarize the financial aspects of the quote or order.

In general, when laying out a quote or order on a CRM screen, the first half of the table is placed at the top of the screen, followed by the list of line items, and then the financial information is placed at the bottom or footer of the screen.

This makes sense because the financial information summates the financial information of the line items, and it therefore should be underneath it.

*SageCRM integration with Sage ERP 100, showing a quote that has been synchronized from ERP to CRM. Most of the quote information is in the top screen, with the line item information in a list below the top screen. Below the list of line item information is the financial information for the quote.*

The preceding screenshot shows a quote that has been synchronized from ERP to CRM. The layout shows the quote information at the top, with the exception of the financial information, which is placed below the list of line items.

The line item fields, which also need to be defined, are shown in the following table:

| ERP order and quote line item fields | ERP field type |
|---|---|
| Document reference | String (12) |
| | This is the unique reference to the quote or order. |
| Line number | Number |
| | This is the unique reference for the order or quote line item. |
| Item code | String (30) |
| | The ERP item code for the item on the line item. |
| UOM | String |
| | The unit of measurement for the item. |
| Quantity | Decimal |
| | The quantity of the item ordered. |
| List price | Decimal |
| | The advertised price for the item. |

| ERP order and quote line item fields | ERP field type |
|---|---|
| Quoted price | Decimal<br><br>The price for the item that is quoted to the customer, which may be different from the list price. |
| Line item discount | Decimal<br><br>The discount that is applied to the line item, if any. |
| Quoted price sum | Decimal<br><br>The sum of quantity multiplied by quoted price minus line item discount. |

The line item table shows the fields and types for each line item on the quote or order. The table is the same whether the line item is for a quote or for an order.

**Make a note**

Some of the fields on the quote or order or line items are calculated fields. For example, the quoted price sum is the sum of quantity multiplied by quoted price minus line item discount on a line item. In order to avoid issues with rounding and precision, it is better to take the value from the ERP, rather than to try to recalculate it on the CRM side.

# Workshop

Define the fields and field types that you will be synchronizing. Create field mapping tables for quotes, orders, and quote and order line items for your CRM to ERP integration.

# Step 5 – defining the CRUD rules

We have defined the entities, the fields, their mappings, and how they will be uniquely identified.

We now need to define the CRUD rules for our synchronization. We need to design the rules for what happens when the entities that we are synchronizing are created, updated, and deleted in both ERP and CRM.

In our worked example, the orders and the quotes that we are synchronizing will be read-only in CRM, and so we only need to define rules for what happens when they are created, updated, or deleted in ERP.

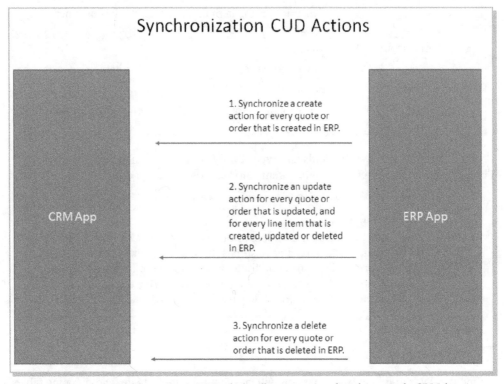

*Create, update, and delete actions in ERP, which will cause corresponding changes in the CRM data*

Create, update, and delete actions in ERP will cause corresponding changes in the CRM data. The synchronization is one way, so there will be no synchronization of data in the other direction.

# Creating quotes, orders, and line items

When a quote or order is created in ERP, the synchronization software will need to detect the new record and create a corresponding quote or order in CRM. The quote or order will have line items, and these will need to be brought over and created in CRM as well. When the records are created, their unique references must be set, and the quote or order must contain a reference to the associated customer.

It is possible to add a new line item to an existing quote or order. This will be treated as a quote or order update.

# Updating quotes or orders

When a quote or order is updated in ERP, the synchronization software will need to detect that the change has occurred and update the corresponding record in CRM.

Line items can be added, updated, or deleted from an existing quote or order. As line items are child entities of a quote or order, this will be treated as an update to a quote or order action.

In some ERP applications, when the line items on a quote or order change, it is difficult to tell what has actually been changed, and so the developer cannot determine what needs to be updated on the CRM side. For example, sometimes if line items are deleted, the line item numbers change for the remaining line items, and therefore the line item numbers cannot be relied upon.

A workaround for this is that whenever the line items on a quote or order change, the synchronization software should delete all the line items for the record in CRM and add them back in again afresh. While this is an inefficient solution from a coding point of view, it makes sure the line items are up to date, with no discrepancies between ERP and CRM, which is important for the CRM users.

# Deleting quotes or orders

When a quote or order is deleted in ERP, the synchronization software will need to detect that the change has occurred and delete the corresponding record in CRM. The line items for the record should be deleted as well.

# Summary of CUD actions

The following table summarizes the CUD actions discussed in this section. It offers an overview of what can happen in ERP to quotes and orders, and of the result that this should trigger in the synchronization software:

| Action in ERP | Synchronization action |
|---|---|
| Create quote or order. | Create corresponding record in CRM. |
| Update quote or order. Create, update, or delete a line item on an existing quote or order. | Update corresponding quote or order in CRM. |
| Delete quote or order. | Delete corresponding record in CRM. |

Now that we have worked through the CUD actions for our worked example, you should do the same for your ERP and CRM application.

# Workshop

Define **Create, Update, and Delete** synchronization rules for quotes, orders, and line items for your CRM to ERP integration.

# Step 6 – designing the screen pops

This is the first time that screen pops will be used as part of a design, since we did not use them in the contact management integration.

Screen pops will be employed by the sales user for creating and updating quotes and orders. The CRM user will be, in effect, using ERP screens to create quotes and orders without having to exit the CRM. This saves development effort because the screens do not have to be re-implemented in CRM. The screen pops will be launched from buttons placed in the CRM UI.

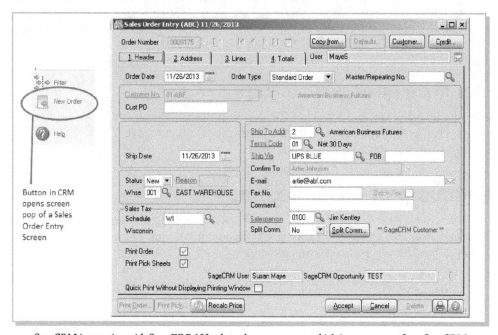

*SageCRM integration with Sage ERP 100 sales order entry screen, which is a screen pop from SageCRM*

When we launch a screen pop, we can choose to create a new quote or order or edit an existing quote or order. We need to pass information to the ERP screen so that it can load correctly and will know in what context to display. The information that needs to be passed is as follows:

> ➤ Authentication for the ERP screen
> ➤ Customer unique reference
> ➤ Quote or order unique reference

# Authentication for the ERP screen

When the ERP screen is loaded, it should already be authenticated so that the user does not need to enter a username and password. The solution for this will be different for every ERP, but in general, the authentication details should be stored somewhere in the CRM application so that they can be passed to the screen pop when it is launched.

# Customer unique reference

When we create a new order or quote, we will be doing it for a customer. We will therefore need to pass the customer's unique reference to the ERP screen, so that the ERP knows which customer to create the new quote or order for. The preceding screenshot shows a new order screen in the SageCRM integration with Sage ERP 100, with the customer "American Business Futures" already filled in. Because the customer name is filled in, other useful default values will be filled in as well, such as the default shipping address, the ship via value, and the sales tax values.

# Quote or order unique reference

When an existing quote or order is to be edited, the screen needs to be passed the quote or order unique reference so that it will display the correct record.

# Linking a quote or order with a CRM user

When a quote or order is synchronized to CRM, it is useful to know which user created it. The information can be used in reports and dashboards to show a user's and a team's sales progress.

When the quote or order is created using the screen popping mechanism, the user will be asked to select their name in the ERP screen, and this information will later be synchronized back to CRM.

*Salesperson field in the Sage ERP 100 order entry screen*

The screen snippet shows the salesperson field in the Sage ERP 100 order entry screen. In order to support this feature, each CRM sales user will need to be registered in the ERP application as a salesperson.

Alternatively, the authentication mechanism for the launch of the screen pop could contain information about the CRM user, so that the salesperson field is automatically filled in. The CRM user will still need to be already registered in the ERP application.

**Tip**

**Accessing the screen pop from outside the firewall**

Users may wish to use the feature from outside the company firewall, particularly if CRM is already available outside the company firewall. The integration developer will need to consider how to launch the screen pop while getting past firewall restrictions. Depending on how the screen pop works, some ports may need to be opened. Care will need to be taken to ensure that there is no security breach. If there are any issues with opening ports, then the feature should not be used outside the company firewall.

# Location of the buttons

The buttons to launch the quote and order screens need to be located in an appropriate place in the CRM UI so that they fit in with the sales user's workflow and they fit in with the quotes and orders that are being synchronized from the ERP. New quote and order buttons are usually located beside a quote or order list screen in the area where the synchronized quotes and orders are displayed. Edit quote and order buttons are usually located on a quote or order details screen in the area where the synchronized quotes and order details are displayed. We will talk more about the location of the buttons in the later section on CRM UI changes.

# Workshop

Design how you will add screen pops to launch quote and order screens for your CRM to ERP integration. What authentication details need to be passed? Can they be used outside the firewall? Can you initialize the screen pop as a new quote or order, and as the edit of an existing quote or order?

# Security

We have defined the entities, how they relate to each other, and how they will be uniquely identified, and we have defined the fields for each entity and how they map between CRM and ERP fields, as well as the CRUD synchronization actions.

Orders and quotes will be new entities in CRM, and, by default, they may have no security, or they may inherit the security of the customers that they are associated with. We need to consider whether additional security restrictions need to be added.

# Orders and quotes that are viewable in CRM

ERP orders and quotes will now be viewable in CRM to all CRM users.

Some approaches to restricting the order and quote data that is shown to your users include:

> **No restriction**: If there is no security, all your CRM users will have access to all ERP quote and order information. This may be acceptable in some implementations.

> **Restrictions based on customer**: Order and quote security could be implemented to inherit the security permissions of the customer that they are associated with. If a CRM user has permission to view a customer, they will also have permission to view the quotes and orders for the customer.

> **Restricting based on user role**: Order and quote security could be implemented so that only users with a sales role can view them.

> **Restricting based on customer and role**: Order and quote security could be implemented so that users must be of the sales role and must be able to view the customer in order to see the quotes and orders for the customer.

# Creating and editing orders and quotes

ERP orders and quotes will now be creatable and editable by using ERP screen pops.

It is advisable to be very careful about which users are allowed to create quotes and orders directly in the ERP application. The same restrictions that you have in your ERP application on quote and order creation should also be applied in CRM.

The users who are able to create and edit quotes and orders can be controlled simply by hiding the button to launch the screen pops from certain categories of users.

Some approaches to hiding the buttons can be:

> **No restriction**: Any user can access a screen with a button and create or edit the quote or order. This is not recommended.

> **Restricting access based on user role or job title**: Only users with certain roles or job titles (for example, inside sales reps only) can create or edit quotes or orders.

> **Restricting access based on customer**: If you are allowed to edit the customer, you should be allowed to create and edit quotes and orders for the customer.

> **A combination of restrictions**: Based on role and access to the customer list, and other areas such as territory, job title, and experience can be considered.

# Security summary

The summary of security areas is shown in the following table:

| Action in CRM | Recommendation |
|---|---|
| Read quotes or orders | Review users with read access, change permissions as necessary |
| Create/update quotes or orders | Review users with create/update access, hide buttons that launch the screen pops as necessary |

In general, the new use cases should be reviewed and access permissions should be modified as necessary.

## Workshop

Decide which CRM users should be allowed to view ERP quote and order information in CRM. Should it be per user, per team, or per user role? How will this be enforced in your CRM?

Decide which CRM users should be allowed to launch quote and order screen pops from CRM. Should it be per user, per team, or per user role? How will this be enforced in your CRM?

# CRM UI changes

We have defined the entities and fields, their mappings, and their security rules. We will now identify the UI changes to CRM that will need to be made for each entity.

In our worked example, the quotes and orders are new entities, and therefore they will appear in new screens. We will put them under the CRM customer context so that a user will locate the quotes and orders by first navigating to a customer.

If your CRM application already has quotes and orders, you will be able to reuse the quotes and orders screens that you already have, but you will need to make them read only so that a CRM user does not change the synchronized quote and order information.

In a workshop section at the end of the chapter, we will consider the costs and benefits of locating quotes and orders under the opportunity context instead of under the customer context.

The navigation paradigm will be as follows:

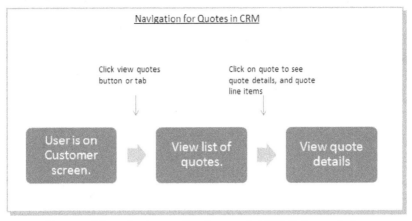

*Diagram of the navigation paradigm for quotes in CRM. Orders are similar.*

The following screens show how this could look in a CRM integration:

*Customer summary screen with quote and order tab in a customized SageCRM integration with Sage ERP 100.*

The preceding screenshot shows a customer summary screen with quote and order tabs. Clicking on the quote or order tabs brings the user to a quote or order list for the customer:

Once the customer has navigated to the quote list, they are shown a list of quotes for the customer. On the right-hand side, there is a **New Quote** button which launches a screen pop for a new quote for the customer. A new quote will be created first in ERP and will then be synchronized to CRM, and will appear on the same quote list.

The list shows basic information for the quote: a quote unique reference, description, and a quote total. The user can click on any of the quotes to go to the quote details screen.

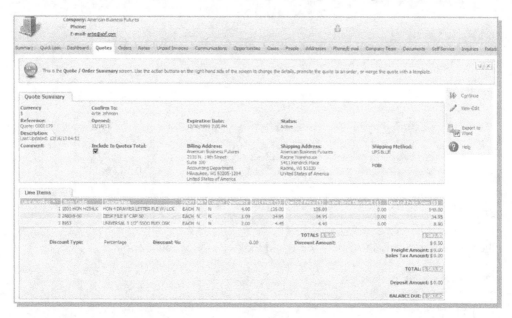

When the user goes to the quote details screen, they are presented with all the information that has been synchronized for the quote and the quote line items. There is an edit quote button on the right-hand side which will launch a screen pop for editing the quote. An edited quote will change first in ERP and then the change is synchronized to CRM, and will appear on the same quote details screen.

# New screens that need to be built

The following list summarizes the new UI screens that need to be built for our sales management integration:

> **Quote and order list screen**: The quote and order list screen will show a list of quotes or orders for the customer. The fields on the list will be a selection of the more useful fields that are synchronized. There will be a button on the list screen which will launch the new quote or order screen pop.

> **Quote and order details screen**: When the user clicks on a quote or order on the quote and order list screen, they will be brought to the quote and order details screen. This will show all the available fields for the quote or order and a list of the line items for the record. There will be a button on the screen which will launch the edit quote or order screen pop.

> **Administration area**: The authentication details to allow for logging into the screen pops may need to be stored in the administration area for the integration.

# Report/dashboard changes

Quote and order information is very valuable for sales reports. Now that they are in CRM, they can be added to existing reports and/or dashboards, or new reports and/or dashboards can be created for them. Some examples of new reports or dashboards that can be created are:

> ➤ Sales reports by customers or by users, team, or territory. There are many different types of report that can be created based on quote and order information linked with the customer information. The reports can show how well your users are doing or how your teams are doing, or they can be created based on geographical territory or business sector.

> ➤ Items ordered by quantity or value grouped by sales user or customer. From the sales order items that are synchronized, it is possible to see how much of each item is ordered, when it was sold, who sold it, and to whom it was sold. There are many different ways to view this data to give you a snapshot of how well different items are being sold.

> ➤ Reports on quote progress versus orders taken. As quotes and orders are in the CRM database, it is possible to analyze them and see information such as what percentage of quotes are converted to orders, who is the best CRM sales user at converting quotes to orders, and the average time to convert a quote to an order.

> ➤ Revenue forecast over a time period such as the next quarter, by user, team, or region. As quote and order information is in CRM, it is possible to use the historic data to do some forecasts for sales in the future. If you have the average time to convert a quote to an order, you can look at existing quotes and predict how many will be converted to an order in the next time period.

# Workshop

Gather all the design work that you have completed for this chapter so far and use the information to compile a list of UI changes that will need to be made.

Define which reports and/or dashboards should be updated or created to make use of the new quote and order data that is available in CRM.

# Advanced workshop discussion

The following advanced workshop questions discuss additional features and solutions that can be considered as part of the sales management integration solution. Evaluate whether you should add the ability to view customer inventory and price list information in CRM.

A common CRM integrated use case is to be able to do a price check or an inventory check on ERP items. In our sales management integration, there is an indirect way of doing this use case, which is to create a quote. The quote will give the correct price for an item and will also inform the user whether the inventory is available.

An alternative solution is to build screens in CRM that show pricing information and inventory information. In order to evaluate this option, the designer should go through all the design steps. A short summary of the important considerations needed for a price check feature is as follows:

> ➤ Define the entities. The entities will include items, prices for items, and inventory for items.

> ➤ Define how to implement the price calculation. In ERP, prices can be calculated on the fly based on various factors such as customer type, item weight, item quantity, item warehouse location, and customer and item tax authority.

> ➤ All the information for calculating a price will need to be synchronized to CRM and code will need to be written to do the calculation in CRM, or else the ERP software API may provide a pricing service that will do the calculation based on a set of parameters such as customer, item, and quantity.

> ➤ Define where to locate the price check on the CRM UI. This could be located in the customer context as a button that launches a new screen.

Once the design has been carried out, the team can evaluate whether it is of sufficient benefit to the CRM user to implement. Evaluate whether you should implement a feature to bulk import all ERP quotes and orders to CRM.

In our contact integration design, we have a feature to do an initial bulk import of all customers from ERP to CRM. A similar feature can be designed for the sales management integration, to bring over all the quotes and orders in ERP that already existed in ERP prior to the implementation of the sales management integration.

The feature would also be useful as a way to occasionally refresh the CRM data, and make sure that all the quotes and orders in CRM had the same information as the quotes and orders in ERP.

The design of this feature is similar to the design of the bulk import of customers from ERP to CRM:

> ➤ A trigger will be needed in the CRM UI to start the bulk import. It could be a button in a CRM administration screen, in the same way as it is for the bulk import of customers. This will trigger a bulk import of quotes and orders. All the quotes and orders in ERP will get copied to CRM. Quotes and orders that already exist in CRM will be updated and quotes and orders that did not already exist in CRM will be newly created.

> ➤ The implementation of the import will depend on which method is used for synchronization.

For your integration, consider whether it is of benefit to build your bulk import feature for quotes and orders. Evaluate whether you should build quotes and orders screens in CRM rather than using screen pops.

In our solution to the sales management integration, we used screen pops for the creation and editing of quotes and orders. An alternative, more costly method is to build the quote and order functionality in CRM.

The advantages of doing this is that the screens are part of CRM, and it can be a more satisfactory user experience. It may be easier to expose the feature through the company firewall, and therefore it helps users who are doing remote working.

However, the screens will be a significant effort to build and maintain.

For your integration, consider whether you would prefer to build your own quote and order screens or use the screen pop option. If your CRM application has opportunities, evaluate whether you should display the imported quotes and orders in the opportunity context rather than the customer context.

The benefit of linking the quotes and orders with opportunities is that your CRM users can use opportunities and seamlessly move to creating quotes and orders from within the opportunity. This leads to a more connected sales workflow. Some of the changes needed are as follows:

> * The screens to list and view quotes and orders will be from the opportunity context rather than the customer context. A user will need to create an opportunity before creating a quote or order.

> * Quotes and orders that are created in ERP from the screen pops, and which are synchronized back to CRM, will need to be linked with the correct opportunity. The integration developer will need to pass the opportunity unique reference to the screen pops so that the quotes and orders that are created in ERP will know which opportunity they are linked to. When the synchronization code synchronizes them to CRM, they will need to be linked with the correct opportunity as well as to the correct customer.

> * Quotes and orders that are created directly in ERP will need to be synchronized into an opportunity as well. A default opportunity will need to be created for each customer, which will be associated with all the quotes and orders that are created directly in ERP.

As you can see, while linking quotes and orders to opportunities is potentially more beneficial to a user, it also comes with a higher development cost. The costs and benefits need to be weighed up for your integration.

# Summary

In this chapter, we designed a sales management integration. We started off by describing a real-world scenario for a fictional business called RideRight Bike Parts Company, which needed to extend its contact management integration by adding a sales management integration.

We identified the uses cases and reframed them as CRM workflows that we needed to implement:

> * The ability to create quotes and orders in CRM
> * The ability to view quote and order history in CRM

We then designed the integration solution using the real-world applications of SageCRM and Sage ERP 300 to provide some context. We followed the same design steps outlined in the previous chapter, with an additional step to design the screen pops. In the workshops, you were asked to follow along using your CRM and ERP applications. We discussed the security implications of the changes we are making. Finally, we summarized the UI customizations that will be required for the sales management integration.

In the advanced workshop section, we discussed additional features and alternative solutions that can be considered:

> ➤ Ability to do a price check or look at inventory information
> ➤ Ability to bulk import all quotes and orders
> ➤ Evaluation of building custom quote and order screens rather than using screen pops
> ➤ How to link ERP quotes and orders with CRM opportunities

At this point, the design is completed for the sales management integration. The next step is to develop the solution. *Chapter 5, How to Build a Collections Management Integration*, talks about the next development stage in more detail.

In the next chapter, we design the collections management integration. The collections management integration is an integration feature to allow CRM users to chase payment of overdue invoices.

# > 5

# How to Build a Collections Management Integration

In previous chapters, we covered the design of a contact management integration and a sales management integration. In this chapter, we will design a collections management integration for sales users to chase overdue invoices.

We will use real-world scenarios for our fictional company, RideRight Bike Parts Company, to build up the use cases. We will then design CRM integrated workflows for those use cases.

In the advanced workshop at the end of the chapter, we will discuss alternative use cases so that you can tailor your integration to suit your particular business needs.

## Collections management integration use cases

RideRight Bike Parts Company has implemented the contact management integration and the sales management integration between their CRM and ERP applications. Their sales users are particularly pleased with the way that they can now do quotes and orders from their CRM application and how this has sped up their workflow and allowed for a higher throughput of sales.

The successful rollout of the integration has prompted management to look further downstream in the sales process to see if any more benefits can be gained from their CRM to ERP integration. They are now focused on using CRM to speed up the payment of invoices and improve the company cash flow.

At RideRight Bikes, invoices are sent out with the bicycle accessories that are sold to their customers. The standard payment terms are 30 days after receipt of invoice. Many customers do not pay after 30 days, some waiting until 15 days later or longer, and some wait until they have been reminded once or twice by RideRight to make a payment. The process for collecting the overdue invoices is haphazard. The accountant goes through the invoices in the ERP and makes phone calls to the customer. A spreadsheet is used to keep a record of who has been called, but it is hard to get an overview of which customers are good at making payments on time and which customers are less reliable with their payments.

When sales users are making sales to customers they do not know if that particular customer has outstanding overdue invoices.

RideRight would like to enhance their integration with CRM to support the following use cases:

> ➤ RideRight would like their sales and customer support users to be able to see the invoice payment status in CRM, for use when making sales and in communication with customers.

> ➤ RideRight would like their CRM users, either sales or support, to be able to chase unpaid invoices using their CRM application. They would like to be able to use different methods to request payment using CRM functionality such as e-mail, phone calls, SMS by phone, letters demanding payment (dunning letters), and to reliably track who they have contacted and who has paid.

> ➤ RideRight would like to be able to see reports and dashboards with overdue customer information. They would like to use this information so that they can reward those customers who pay on time, and offer incentives to late payers, such as discounts of 2% to 5% on future timely payments.

# Integration workflows

The use cases that are required for collections management can be converted to a new integration workflow:

> ➤ Ability to view ERP invoices in CRM, including:

>> ➢ Ability to use invoice information when using the CRM interaction feature (for example, phone-call management, e-mail management, document management, and so on)

>> ➢ Ability to view invoice information in CRM reports and dashboards

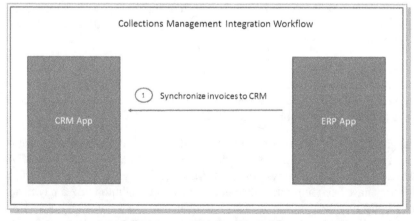

*Collections manager integration workflow*

# Ability to view ERP invoices in CRM

When employees of RideRight want to chase overdue invoices to improve the company cash flow they have to use the ERP application and informal tracking methods such as spreadsheets or paper records to track whom they have contacted. They have poor visibility on how well they are doing at collecting overdue invoices. It is difficult to manage the process and make improvements.

The workflow will be changed so that CRM users will be able to chase overdue invoices using CRM functionality, which is specifically designed for managing and tracking communications with customers. CRM managers will be able to measure the success of their payment collection process through CRM reports and dashboards, and they will be able to reward good customers and incentivize customers with a poor record of payment.

# How

ERP invoices will be one-way synchronized from ERP to CRM. They will be read only in CRM. The invoice feature in CRM will be integrated with the CRM interactions feature so that CRM users will be able to take full advantage of the CRM interactions functionality in chasing unpaid invoices.

CRM reports and dashboards will be created to show collections management KPI information, based on the ERP invoice data, which will allow CRM users to easily analyze the progress of their collections workflow.

## Design step 1 – creating entity diagrams

The workflow for the collections integration has been defined. We will now go through our design steps, starting with step one: creating entity diagrams. We will use the real-world applications of Sage CRM and Sage ERP 300 in our examples so that it is a realistic design. You will be asked to design the solution for your own ERP and CRM in workshop sections throughout the chapter.

Invoices do not exist in CRM. We must therefore make an entity diagram for invoices in ERP and create corresponding new invoice entities in CRM.

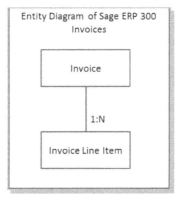

*Entity diagram for invoices and invoice line items*

The preceding diagram shows the entity diagram for invoices and invoice line items. Invoices have line items in the same way that quotes and orders have line items. There is a line item for every item that is sold on the invoice showing the item, the quantity sold, and the actual price.

# Design step 2 – mapping the entity diagrams to each other

The next step allows us to work out how we will deal with the differences in the entity relationships between CRM and ERP.

| Entity | Mapping rule |
| --- | --- |
| Invoice | Each invoice in CRM will map to an invoice in ERP |
| Invoice line item | Each invoice line item in CRM will map to an invoice line item in ERP |

In this example, as invoices and invoice line items do not exist in CRM, we will need to create invoice and invoice line item entities in CRM that will match the entities in ERP. If your CRM application already has invoices, instead of creating a new invoice entity you will need to map the invoices in ERP to the invoices in CRM. This is a similar task to the exercise in the previous chapter where we created quote and order entities in CRM.

# Design step 3 – defining the unique identifiers

Now that we have defined the entities and the rules for how they will map to each other, we need to define how we will uniquely identify every record that we are synchronizing. The preferred method is to use the unique identifiers in the ERP database if they are available. If they are not available, use the invoice reference number.

## Unique Identifiers for Invoices

Unique
identifier for
invoices

Unique
identifier for
invoice line
items

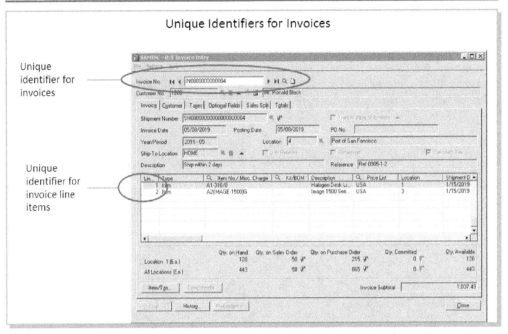

*Unique identifiers for invoices are the invoice reference number, and for invoice line items they are the invoice line number*

For our example we will use the invoice reference number. Invoices also need to be associated with a customer. We will use the customer number field on the invoice to link it with the correct customer. It is also useful to bring over the salesperson field so that the invoice can be associated with a CRM user if there is one.

The line items are children of the invoice, and they can be uniquely identified by a combination of their parent invoice reference number and their line number.

---

**Tip**

**Workshop**

Do an entity relationship diagram for invoices in your ERP.

Define the unique references for the invoices and line items in your ERP.

---

# Design step 4 – defining the fields and field mappings

We have defined the entities, their mapping, and how they will be uniquely identified.

The next step is to identify which invoice fields we will be synchronizing. We also need to gather field characteristics such as type and size. The fields do not exist in CRM. We will therefore do this exercise for the ERP fields, and then we'll create identical fields in CRM to map them to.

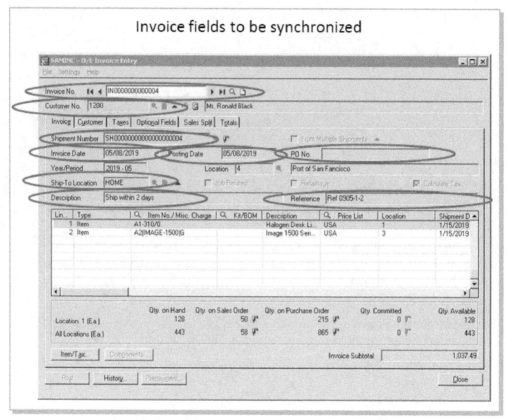

*Screenshot of Sage ERP 300 invoice showing fields to be synchronized*

We start by looking at the invoice UI in ERP and picking which fields we would like to bring to CRM. The previous screen shows a Sage ERP 300 invoice details screen with some of the fields that we would like to synchronize circled.

The table below shows the invoice fields that should be synchronized to CRM.

| ERP invoice fields | ERP field type |
|---|---|
| Invoice number | String (12)<br><br>Note that this is the unique reference for the invoice. |
| Customer number | String (12)<br><br>Note that this is the unique reference to a customer. We use this field to associate an invoice to a customer. |
| Description | String (60) |
| Invoice date | Date |
| Actual ship date | Date<br><br>The date the items were shipped. |
| Currency | String (5)<br><br>This tells which currency the invoice is in, and is useful if we are dealing with a multi currency system. |
| Sales Person | String (60)<br><br>The name of the sales user. If this is the same name as a CRM user, the invoice can be linked with a CRM user, which is useful for reporting. |
| PO Number | String (30)<br><br>Purchase order number. A reference to the purchase order if one exists. |
| Ship-To Location | String (30)<br><br>A reference to the location that the shipment was shipped to. |
| **Financial information** | |
| Invoice subtotal | Decimal<br><br>The sum of all the line item price sum values, see line item fields. |
| Discount amount | Decimal |
| Miscellaneous charges total | Decimal |
| Total tax | Decimal |
| Prepayment amount | Decimal |
| Amount due | Decimal<br><br>The sum of invoice subtotal, discount amount, miscellaneous charges, total tax, minus prepayment amount. |

*Table of invoice fields that are to be synchronized*

The fields of an invoice contain general information about the invoice such as description, customer number, and opened date, and they contain financial information about the invoice, such as total tax, discount amounts, and amount due. The only financial field that is strictly necessary is the amount due field, which tells you how much is outstanding on the invoice, but the other financial fields are useful for the CRM users to have in case they get asked questions about the invoice.

We also need to define the fields on the invoice line item. The line item fields are defined in the following table:

| ERP Invoice Line Item Fields | ERP Field Type |
|---|---|
| Invoice Number | String (12)<br>This is the unique reference to the invoice. |
| Line Number | Number<br>This is the unique reference for the invoice line item. |
| Item Code | String (30)<br>The ERP item code for the item on the line item. |
| UOM | String<br>The Unit of Measure for the item. |
| Quantity | Decimal<br>The quantity of the item invoiced. |
| Item Price | Decimal<br>The price for the item that is invoiced to the customer. |
| Line Item Discount | Decimal<br>The discount that is applied to the line item, if any. |
| Line Item Price Sum | Decimal<br>The sum of Quantity multiplied by Item Price minus Line Item Discount. |

The invoice line item table shows the fields and types for each line item on the invoice that is to be synchronized.

As with quotes and orders, some of the fields on the invoice and invoice line items are calculated fields. For example, the line item price sum is calculated as the sum of the quantity of the line item multiplied by the item price, minus any discounts. In order to avoid issues with rounding and precision, it is better to take the calculated value from the ERP rather than to try to recalculate it on the CRM side.

**Tip**

**Workshop**

Define the fields and field types that you will be synchronizing for invoices.

# Design step 5 – defining the CRUD rules

We have defined the entities, the fields, their mappings, and how they will be uniquely identified. We now need to define the CRUD rules for our synchronization. In our example, the invoices that we are synchronizing will be read only in CRM and so we only need to define rules for what happens when they are created, updated, or deleted in ERP.

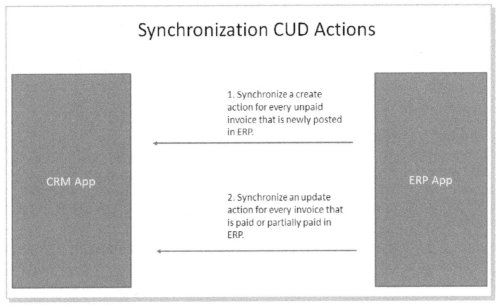

*Diagram showing the synchronization CUD actions for the invoices that we are synchronizing*

The preceding diagram shows the synchronization CUD actions for the invoices that we are synchronizing. Create and update actions in ERP will cause corresponding changes in the CRM data. The synchronization is one way, so there will be no synchronization of data in the other direction.

## Creating invoice and invoice line items

We are mainly interested in invoices that are overdue, so for this use case we will only synchronize invoices that have been posted in the ERP application.

When an invoice is newly posted in ERP, the synchronization software will need to detect that a new record has been created and create a corresponding invoice in CRM. The invoice will have line items, and these will need to be brought over and created in CRM as well. When the records are created, their unique references must be set. The invoice must also contain a reference to the associated customer.

If we would like to reduce the number of invoices that are synchronized to CRM, there are two tactics that we can consider:

> ➤ Instead of transferring all posted invoices, we could filter for invoices that have a positive balance. We can do this because we are only interested in invoices that have not been paid yet. Invoices with a zero balance have already been paid. For our worked example we will use this design.

> ➤ Instead of bringing over all newly created posted invoices we could filter for invoices that are over 30 days old and are still unpaid. Assuming that some invoices are paid in the first 30 days after they are posted, this will further reduce the number of invoices that are brought over. For our example we will not use this design because we would like to see all the unpaid invoices from the time that they are opened.

# Updating invoices

Invoice updates are simpler to handle than updates to quotes or orders because, typically, the only update to an invoice is to indicate that it has been paid, or partially paid. The 'amount due' field is the only field that will change. When the invoice is fully paid, the amount due will be zero. Invoice line items fields are not expected to change after they are created.

When the 'amount due' field of an invoice changes in ERP, the synchronization software will need to detect that the change has occurred and update the corresponding invoice record in CRM.

# Deleting invoices

It is not expected that posted invoices will be deleted. If they can be deleted (or voided) in your ERP you will need to make sure that the synchronization takes care of deleted invoices. Alternatively, you can simply update the invoice in CRM so that the amount due is equal to zero.

# Summary of CUD actions

The following table shows the summary of the actions that can happen in ERP to invoices, and what they will trigger in the synchronization software.

| Action in ERP | Synchronization action |
| --- | --- |
| Create invoice by posting an invoice in ERP. | If the invoice is unpaid, and therefore has an 'amount due' value greater than zero, create a corresponding invoice record in CRM. |
| Update to invoice. The amount due for the invoice will change. | Update the amount due field for the corresponding invoice in CRM. |

**Tip**

**Workshop**

Define Create, Update, and Delete synchronization rules for invoices for your collections management integration.

# Security

ERP invoices will now be viewable in CRM to CRM users. By default, they may have no security restrictions, or they may inherit the security of the customers with which they are associated. We need to consider if additional security restrictions need to be added.

Some approaches to restricting the invoice data that is shown to your users include:

> **No restriction**: If there is no security, all your CRM users will have access to all the invoices that are synchronized to CRM. This may be acceptable in some implementations.

> **Restricting based on customer**: Invoice security can be implemented to inherit the security permissions of the customer with which they are associated. If a CRM user has permission to view a customer, they will also have permission to view the invoices for the customer.

> **Restricting based on user role**: Invoice security can be implemented so that, for example, only users with a sales role or a support role can view them.

> **Restricting based on customer and role**: Invoice security can be implemented so that users must be of a certain role *and* must be able to view the customer associated with the invoice in order to see an invoice. For example, only sales users who have permissions to view a customer will be able to see the invoices for that customer.

**Tip**

**Workshop**

Decide the security rules for your invoices.

# CRM UI changes

In our worked example, invoices are new entities and therefore they will appear in new screens. The navigation paradigm will be as follows:

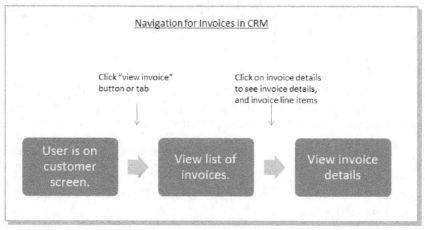

*The Navigation paradigm for invoices in CRM*

The following screenshot show how this could look in a CRM integration:

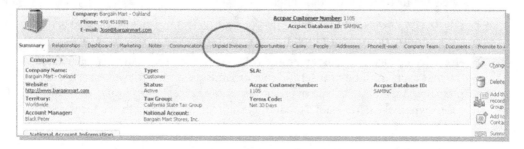

A customer summary screen with unpaid invoice tab in a customized Sage CRM integration with Sage ERP 300. Clicking on the unpaid invoice tab brings the user to a list of invoices that have not yet been paid for the customer.

The preceding screenshot shows a customer summary screen with an unpaid invoices tab. Clicking on the unpaid invoices tab brings the user to a list of unpaid invoices for the customer.

*Screenshot of a list of invoices for a customer in a customized Sage CRM integration with Sage ERP 300. Clicking on an invoice will bring the customer to the invoice details page.*

Once the CRM user has navigated to the invoice list, they are shown a list of invoices for the customer.

The preceding screenshot shows a list of invoices in a customized Sage CRM integration with Sage ERP 300. On the right-hand-side is a range of filter options allowing the user to filter by fields such as due date, amount due, and status. There are a number of other features on the screen that are discussed later in the book:

> ➤ It is possible to filter by aged status. This is discussed in the *Advanced workshop* section of this chapter.

> ➤ It is possible to filter by the ERP company database. Support for multiple ERP databases is discussed in a later chapter in this book.

> ➤ It is possible to filter by status and stage—these are CRM fields that support the CRM workflow feature. We will talk about this in the *Advanced workshop* section.

The user can click on any of the invoices to go to the invoice details screen:

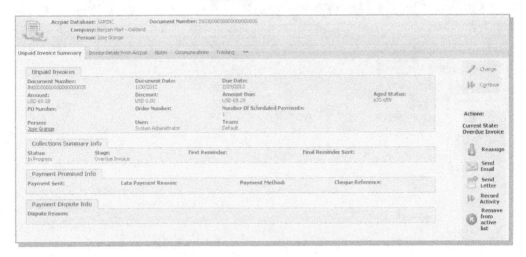

This screenshot does not show invoice line items as they were not included in this customization.

When the user goes to the invoice details screen, they are presented with all the information that has been synchronized for the invoice. The previous screenshot shows the invoice details for a customized SageCRM integration with Sage ERP 300. The screen also shows some CRM specific data to allow for CRM workflow. This is discussed in the advanced workflow section of the chapter.

# New screens that need to be built

We have discussed the UI changes that are needed using some examples and screenshots. A summary of the new screens that need to be built for your CRM application is as follows:

> **Invoice list screen**: The invoice lists will show a list of invoices for the customer. The fields on the list will be a selection of the more useful fields that are synchronized.

> **Invoice details screen**: When the user clicks on an invoice on the invoice list screen they will be brought to the invoice details screen. This will show all the available fields for the invoice.

The screens that are shown in the screenshots above show links to e-mail management, letter sending, and other communications management. These links connect the invoice feature with the CRM interactions functionality, which is an important goal for the integration because it allows CRM users to use the CRM interactions functionality when chasing invoice payments. The integration developer should design their new UI screens so that they are linked with the CRM interactions functionality.

# Reports/dashboard changes

Reports and dashboards are useful tools for measuring the success of the collections management feature. Some examples of new reports or dashboards that can be created are:

> ➤ A list of all customers who owe money, ordered by size of debt

> ➤ A list of all customers who have had invoices outstanding for more than 30 days

> ➤ Outstanding invoices by size of amount due, or opened date, or by aged status (see *Advanced workshop*)

> ➤ Customers who have recently paid an invoice

In the workshop section, you will have the opportunity to design your own reports and dashboards to suit your particular business needs for collections management.

---

**Tip**

**Workshop**

Gather together all the design work that you have completed for this chapter so far and use the information to compile a list of UI changes that will need to be made.

Define which reports and/or dashboards should be updated or created to make use of the new invoice data which is available in CRM.

---

# Advanced workshop checklist

> ➤ **Evaluate if it is worthwhile to synchronize more invoice payment information**: In order to get a full view of the debt status of your customer, you need to look at all the posted transactions for the customer, including invoices, debit notes, credit notes, interest, unapplied cash, prepayments, receipts, and refunds. Sometimes this information is stored in the same ERP view or table, and so it is not a major change in the synchronization logic to add on the one-way synchronization of all posted transactions. The drawback is that it will involve copying significantly more information to your CRM database, the time taken to do a synchronization will be longer, and the UIs will need to be updated to show the additional data. Consider whether it is worth the implementation effort to synchronize all posted transactions for the collections management integration feature.

➤ **Consider putting Aging into the CRM application**: Your ERP probably has an Aging report which shows how many of your invoices have been open for 30, 60, or 90 days. The value of the number of days, or **aging buckets**, can be configured manually by an ERP user. You can set up a similar feature in CRM to show the aging for the invoices that have been synchronized to CRM. This feature would allow the CRM user to set up the aging buckets, and then run reports and dashboard gadgets that show the invoices grouped under them:

| Aging Period ••• | | |
|---|---|---|
| **4 Aging Periods Found, Page 1 of 1** | | New |
| **Name** | **From** ▲ | **Date To Age By** |
| 0-29 | 0 | Age By Document Date |
| 30-59 | 30 | Age By Document Date |
| 60-89 | 60 | Age By Document Date |
| 90+ | 90 | Age By Document Date |

*SageCRM integrated with Sage ERP 300 customized with collections management feature showing the Aging period configuration screen*

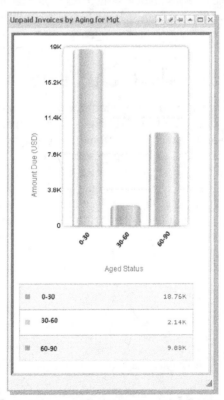

*Sage CRM integrated with Sage ERP 300 customized with collections management feature showing dashboard gadget with invoice Aging summary*

Aging reports are a useful tool to determine the health of a company's cash flow. Consider whether it is of benefit to add it to your collections management integration.

➤ **Evaluate using a bulk import of invoices, both as a way of bringing over all the unpaid invoices at the start of the integration and also as an alternative to synchronization**: With the contact management integration and the sales management integration we considered the benefits of doing a bulk import of the synchronized data, both as a way to start off the integration and as a feature that can be run occasionally to make sure that all the data is correctly synchronized. The same bulk import can be considered for the collections management integration. If collections management is a task that will be run infrequently in CRM, it is also useful to consider doing bulk import of invoices instead of implementing the synchronization of invoices. For example if collections management is done only on Monday afternoons, do the bulk import of invoices on the Monday morning. There is no need to keep the invoices up to date for the rest of the week. This only works if collections are only done at certain preplanned times. The bulk import would need to read all the unpaid posted invoices in ERP and copy them to CRM. If the invoice already exists in CRM, it should be updated. If the invoice does not already exist in CRM, a new invoice should be created. At the end of the bulk import there should be a check of which invoices are in CRM that were not updated during the bulk import. These invoices are invoices that have been paid, and their amount due field should be updated to zero in CRM.

➤ **Consider only bringing over the invoice header as a way to save time**: In the invoice details screenshot of the collections feature that was added to the SageCRM integration with Sage ERP 300 as a customization, there are no invoice line items. That is because it was determined that the invoice header information was adequate for the feature. (The invoice line item information is available elsewhere in that integration as a screen pop.) If you only synchronized invoice header information you will still get useful information such as the amount due, but you will not be able to see invoice line item information. Consider whether you need to synchronize invoice line item information. If you do not, you can save some implementation time by not supporting it.

➤ **Evaluate if you can add CRM workflow to the collections management feature**: In the invoice details screenshot of the collections feature that was added to the SageCRM integration with Sage ERP 300 as a customization, there are some buttons related to CRM workflow. In that implementation, a workflow is implemented to allow the user to change the state of the invoice in CRM based on whether or not certain actions to collect the invoice have been undertaken. This helps users report on the collections' progress. There are also buttons that allow for the quick sending of an e-mail based on an e-mail template, and the quick printing of a dunning letter based on a document template. In addition there are notifications that appear on the screen if a request to pay the invoice has been made and there has been no payment in x number of days. The collections management feature can be made more powerful if it can take full advantage of the native CRM functionality such as workflow, notifications, and escalations. Consider whether you can do this for your CRM.

# Summary

In this chapter, we designed a collections management integration.

We started off by describing a real-world scenario for a fictional business called RideRight Bike Parts Company, which had a need for better collections management to improve cash flow. We identified the use cases and reframed them as CRM workflows that we needed to implement:

> - Ability to view ERP invoices in CRM, including:
>
>   > - Ability to use invoice information when using CRM interactions feature
>   > - Ability to view invoice information in CRM reports and dashboards

We then designed the integration solution using the real-world applications of SageCRM and Sage ERP 300 to provide some context. We followed the same design steps outlined in the previous chapters. In the workshops, the reader was asked to follow along using their CRM and ERP applications.

We discussed the security implications of the changes we are making. Finally we summarized the UI customizations that will be required for the collections management integration.

In the advanced workshop section, we discussed additional features and alternative solutions that can be considered:

> - Ability to synchronize all posted documents rather than just invoices
> - Ability to put Aging reports into the CRM application
> - Ability to do a bulk import of invoices as well as, or instead of, the synchronization
> - Ability to only bring over the invoice header as a way to save time
> - Ability to add CRM workflow to the collections management feature

At this point the design is completed for the collections management integration. The next step is to develop the solution. The chapter called "*How to Develop and Maintain an Integration*" talks about the next development stage in more detail. In the next chapter we will design the **VMI** (**Vendor Management Integration**). The Vendor Management Integration is an integration feature to allow CRM to be used as a simple **VRM** (**Vendor Resource Management**) tool to manage vendors as well as customers.

# > 6

# How to Build a Vendor Management Integration

In previous chapters, we designed contact management, sales management, and collections management integrations. All the integrations had one feature in common: they made use of synchronized customers, or as they are called in the ERP, **accounts receivable customers**.

This chapter will also focus on the benefits of synchronizing vendors, or **accounts payable vendors**, for use by users of the CRM application.

There is a class of applications called **vendor relationship management** (or supplier relationship management), which is for managing vendors. VRM (or SRM) applications can include specialized features for dealing with vendors to help with complex bid negotiation and evaluation. We will not attempt to duplicate a full VRM system. Instead, we will build a simpler alternative, by bringing vendor records from ERP to CRM and integrating them with CRM functionality. Using your CRM application to manage your vendor relationships adds value to your business by enabling stronger, deeper relationships, and hence more valuable business dealings with your vendors.

## Vendor management integration use cases

RideRight Bike Parts Company has implemented contact management integration. The sales and support team are very happy with the way they can see accurate customer information in their CRM.

This contrasts with the RideRight purchasing team. RideRight has a small but busy purchasing team, which deals with purchasing the goods that RideRight sells: bicycle accessories from a range of suppliers in Asia. The purchasing team does not have a vendor relationship management application. Instead, they use ERP and spreadsheets. They find that this is a haphazard way to manage their suppliers. They would like to be able to use CRM-like functionality to help them in their day-to-day workflows. The requirements of the purchasing team are listed here:

> ➤ The RideRight purchasing team would like to be able to use the CRM interactions functionality such as e-mail, phone calls, appointments, and document templates to help them manage their communications with their suppliers. In particular, they would like to be able to use the document management feature to manage their RFPs (request for proposals) and document templates that they send out to vendors. They would like to use the e-mail feature to manage e-mail templates so that they send out consistent information to their vendors.

> ➤ The RideRight purchasing team would like to be able to see a history of their interactions with their vendors, as a way to help resolve vendor queries and potential disputes.

> ➤ The RideRight purchasing manager would like to be able to see reports and dashboards to analyze how the relationships with their vendors are progressing, and to be able to use their vendor data to provide some levels of vendor ranking.

# Integration workflows

The use cases that are required for the RideRight purchasing team can once again be converted to new integration workflows, as we did with the needs of the other teams in previous chapters:

> ➤ Ability to view ERP vendors in CRM, including:
>> ➤ Ability to use the CRM interactions feature for vendors
>> ➤ Ability to view vendor analysis information in CRM reports and dashboards

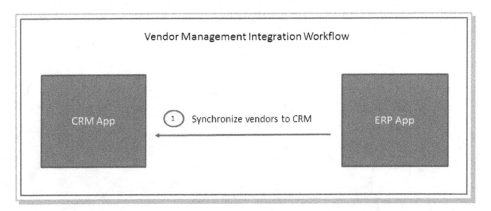

# Ability to view ERP vendors in CRM

The RideRight purchasing team are unable to manage their vendor relationships in an effective and productive way. They currently manage vendor relationships by using the ERP and ad hoc methods such as spreadsheets and e-mail applications.

Their workflow will be changed so that they will use CRM as their primary tool for managing their vendor relationships. They will view vendor information in CRM. They will use the CRM interactions feature, such as e-mail management, document management, and appointment management, to manage communications with their vendors. The interactions feature will display previous and planned interactions with the vendors for tracking purposes. The purchasing manager will be able to use CRM reports and dashboards to analyze the vendor relationships.

# How?

We currently synchronize ERP customers to CRM. We will synchronize ERP vendors to CRM as well. This will allow the purchasing team to manage their work as efficiently and effectively as the sales team.

In order to simplify the integration, vendors can be made read-only in CRM, which means that we only need to be concerned about synchronizing changes to vendors on the ERP side.

In ERP, vendors are shown on different screens to customers, and vendor records can be stored in different database tables to customer records. However, they are very similar entities and have similar data structures. In CRM, vendors can be shown on the same screens as customers, and vendor records can be stored in the same database tables as customer records. This will save having to create new screens and new schema. Vendors will be given a new type in CRM, called "ERP vendor", to distinguish them from ERP customers, which have the type "ERP customer".

The CRM interactions feature is designed to work with customers in CRM. As vendors will be shown on the same screens as CRM customers, albeit with a new type, they will automatically be linked with the CRM interactions feature. New reports and dashboards will be created for vendors to provide KPI information for the vendor data.

## Design step 1 – creating entity diagrams

The workflow for the vendor integration has been defined. We will now go through our design steps, once again starting with step one: creating entity diagrams. As in the previous chapters, we will use the real-world applications of Sage CRM and Sage ERP 300, so that you can see how this process is likely to unfold.

The entity diagram for a vendor is the same as the entity diagram for a customer, except that instead of synchronizing an entity called **customer** we are synchronizing an entity called **vendor**. We can use the same rules as we did for the contact integration.

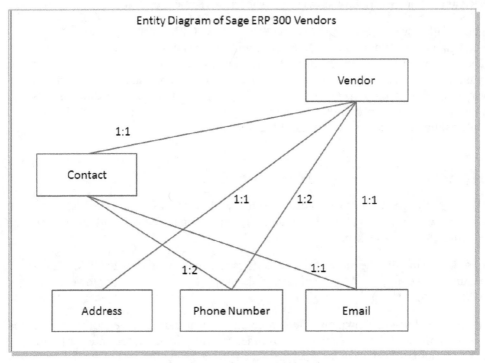

*Entity diagram of Sage ERP 300 vendor*

In our worked example, a vendor has one contact, one address, one e-mail address, and two phone numbers (one of which is a fax number). A contact has one e-mail address and two phone contact numbers.

We also need to do the entity diagram for customers in Sage CRM. This was done in *Chapter 3, How to Build a Contact Integration*, for contact management integration.

---

**Action Point**

**Workshop**

Create an entity relationship diagram for vendors in your ERP.

---

# Design step 2 – mapping the entity diagrams to each other

The vendor entity is very similar to the customer entity. The mapping of the entities will match the mappings used for customers in the contact management integration.

Vendors that are synchronized from ERP will need to be clearly differentiated in CRM from customers that are synchronized from ERP. This can be done by defining a new type in CRM called **ERP vendor**. Vendor records can be assigned to this type.

The contact, address, phone number, and e-mail child entities will have a one-to-one mapping from ERP to CRM:

| Entity | Mapping rule |
|---|---|
| Vendor | ERP vendors will map to CRM customers of type "ERP vendor". |
| Contact | ERP vendor contacts will map to CRM contacts of type "ERP vendor contact". |
| Address | ERP vendor addresses will map to CRM addresses of type "ERP vendor address". |
| Phone number | ERP phone numbers will map to CRM phone numbers of type "ERP vendor phone number". |
| E-mail address | ERP e-mail addresses will map to CRM e-mail addresses of type "ERP vendor e-mail address". |

Note that the vendor data needs to be read-only in the CRM application. For example, a vendor contact will be read-only whereas a CRM native contact will be editable, and similarly for the other child data. This needs to be enforced in the CRM UI business rules. If it helps with the implementation, the child data for a vendor can be given a vendor type during the synchronization. For example, vendor contacts could have a type "ERP vendor contact", and so on. This will help the integration developer write conditional code to make the screens read-only based on a type value for the record. This has been added in the preceding table.

These mappings will allow vendor records to be brought from ERP to CRM and become visible to CRM users so that they can manage their vendor accounts better from the CRM application.

**Tip**

**Workshop**

Define the entity mappings for vendors, and child entities of a vendor, for your ERP and CRM application.

# Design step 3 – defining the unique identifiers

In this worked example, the unique identifier for the vendor will be the vendor number.

*Sage ERP 300 screenshot of a vendor with the vendor number circled, which will be used as the unique reference*

Only the parent entity needs to be identified with a reference number. The child entities will be uniquely identified using a combination of the parent/child relationships between the child data and the parent vendor record and the vendor's reference number. For example, a vendor's contact will be uniquely identified by looking for a contact of type "ERP vendor contact", with the vendor's reference number. There will only be one contact for the vendor, and so the search will return one contact:

| Entity | Unique identifier |
|---|---|
| Vendor | Vendor reference number - this needs to be copied from the ERP to CRM for every vendor that is synchronized. |
| Contact | Use the parent/child relationship between the contact and vendor. The contact will be the only contact of type "ERP vendor contact" associated with the vendor's reference number. |
| Address | Use the parent/child relationship between the address and vendor. The address will be the only address of type "ERP vendor address" associated with the vendor's reference number. |
| Phone number | Use the parent/child relationship between the address and vendor. The phone number will be a phone number of type "ERP phone number" associated with the vendor's reference number. There will be one fax number and one phone number. |
| E-mail address | Use the parent/child relationship between the e-mail address and vendor or contact. The e-mail address will be the only e-mail address associated with the vendor or the contact. |

**Tip**

**Workshop**

Define the unique identifiers for the vendor and child entity records for your ERP and CRM application.

# Design step 4 – defining the fields and field mappings

As in our previous integration examples, the next step of our synchronization design is to define a list of the ERP vendor fields that are to be synchronized and map them to CRM customer fields. This gives us a place to put the ERP vendor data that we are going to synchronize into the CRM application. The vendor fields can be determined by looking at the ERP UI, and by consulting with the purchasing team to see which fields are useful in CRM.

The following table shows the list of vendor fields and field types from our worked example mapped to CRM fields:

| ERP vendor fields | ERP field type | CRM customer field | CRM customer field type |
|---|---|---|---|
| Vendor number | String (length 12)<br><br>Note: this is a special field as it is our unique identifier | Company reference | String (length 12) |
| Vendor name | String (length 60) | Company name | String (length 50) |
| Group code | String (length 6) | - | |
| Short name | String (length 10) | - | |

| ERP vendor fields | ERP field type | CRM customer field | CRM customer field type |
|---|---|---|---|
| Terms code | String (length 6) | - | |
| Tax group | String (length 6) | - | |
| Credit limit | Decimal | - | |
| Credit on hold Status | Checkbox | - | |
| Active/inactive status | Checkbox | - | |
| - | - | Type | String<br><br>Note: this must be set to type = "ERP Vendor" |

In general, the important data to synchronize is data that will be used by the CRM purchasing team when communicating with the vendor. This includes information such as data that identifies the vendor, contact detail information, and some basic status information.

Note that there are "special" fields in the table; the vendor number is used as the unique reference for a vendor record, and the type field in CRM has to be set to "ERP vendor" for every vendor record in order to distinguish the record from ERP customer records and native CRM data that is stored in the same table.

Only two CRM fields already exist in the CRM schema, the company name and the type field. The other fields are non-native CRM fields, but they should already have been created for our contact management integration.

A vendor entity also has child entities: contact, address, phone number, and e-mail address. The fields and mappings for the child entities are the same as the ones that are used for the contact management integration with the exception that the type will be a vendor type rather than a customer type.

The contact entity mapping is shown as an example in the following table. The other child entities can be determined by referring to the contact management integration field mappings section:

| ERP contact fields | ERP field type | CRM contact field | CRM field type |
| --- | --- | --- | --- |
| Contact name | String (length 60) | First name | String (60) |
| | | Last name | String (60) |
| - | - | - | Parent reference<br><br>Note: this is a special field to link the contact with the vendor reference |
| - | - | Type | String<br><br>Note: this must be set to type = "ERP Vendor Contact" |

The "special" fields in the vendor contact are the **vendor reference field**, which is for the vendor reference number and is used to associate the contact with its parent vendor, and the type field, which can be set to **ERP vendor contact**. Both of these fields should already exist in CRM from the contact management integration.

In summary, the fields and mappings for the vendor entity and its child entities are very similar to the mappings for an ERP customer. The schema that has been set up for the ERP customer synchronization should be mostly reusable for the ERP vendor synchronization.

**Tip**

**Workshop**

Define the fields and field mappings for the vendor entity and child entities for your CRM and ERP applications.

# Design step 5 – defining the CRUD rules

We have defined the entities, the fields, their mappings, and how they will be uniquely identified. We now need to define the CRUD rules for our vendor synchronization. In our worked example, the vendors that we are synchronizing will be read-only in CRM, and so we only need to define rules for what happens when they are created, updated, or deleted in ERP.

As with any entity that has child entities, we need to consider not only when the parent entity is created, updated, or deleted, but also when any of the child entities are created, updated, or deleted.

We summarize the synchronization CUD actions in the following diagram, and we will then discuss them in more detail:

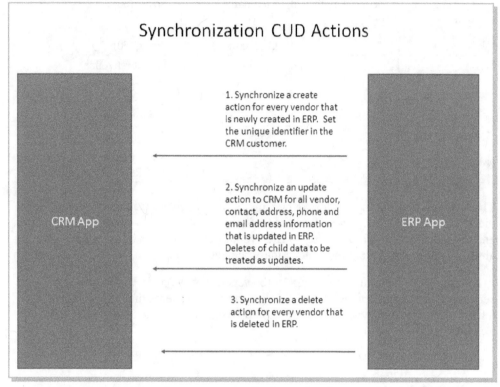

Synchronization CUD Actions

1. Synchronize a create action for every vendor that is newly created in ERP. Set the unique identifier in the CRM customer.

2. Synchronize an update action to CRM for all vendor, contact, address, phone and email address information that is updated in ERP. Deletes of child data to be treated as updates.

3. Synchronize a delete action for every vendor that is deleted in ERP.

CRM App

ERP App

*Summary of CUD synchronization actions, for when vendor information changes in ERP*

## Synchronization of create actions

When a vendor is created in ERP, the synchronization software will need to pick up the record and create a corresponding vendor record in CRM, including corresponding contact, address, phone number, and e-mail information. The unique reference for the vendor record needs to be added to the CRM vendor.

If a vendor is created with some child entity data missing (for example, with no contact data), the implementer has the option of creating a vendor in CRM with no contact child entity or creating a vendor in CRM with a contact child entity that has blank first and last name fields. The difference between the two options is that with the former solution, the implementer will need to support the use case of the contact being created later on, whereas with the latter option, the implementer can support a new contact being added to ERP as a synchronization update use case, where the blank contact name in CRM is filled in.

A similar option exists for all the other child entities. The latter option is simpler to implement as there are less use cases to support. Both creating and updating child entities in ERP will result in a synchronization update to the corresponding CRM entity. For our worked example, we will create all the child records at the same time as the vendor record, leaving the information blank if there is no child entity data.

## Synchronization of update actions

When a vendor is updated in ERP, the synchronization software will need to synchronize the change to CRM as an update to the vendor and/or the child entities; contact, address, phone number, or e-mail address.

The update of a vendor will include when child entity information is added to the vendor, such as when contact information is filled in or an address or phone number is added to a vendor. These will be treated as synchronization updates to the vendor record.

When child entity data is deleted, such as when a contact name is removed, this will also be treated as a synchronization update. When a contact name is removed from a vendor record in ERP, the synchronization software will update the vendor in CRM, blanking out the contact name. Similar rules apply for the other child entity data.

## Synchronization of delete actions

When a vendor record is deleted in ERP, the synchronization software will delete the corresponding vendor in CRM as well as all the child entity data. However, when child entity data is deleted in ERP, such as when a contact name is deleted from a vendor, this will be treated as a synchronization update to the vendor, as discussed in the previous *Synchronization of update actions* section.

**Tip**

**Workshop**

Define, create, update, and delete synchronization rules for vendors and vendor child entity data, including contacts, addresses, phone numbers, and e-mail addresses for your CRM to ERP integration.

# Security

By default, if no new security rules are implemented, any CRM user who is allowed to view companies in CRM will be able to view the ERP vendor list, and may also be able to export the vendor list and use standard CRM interaction functionality with vendors. This needs to be reviewed to make sure that the correct user groups have access to the appropriate actions in CRM.

Some options available are:

> **No restriction**: You could decide that you are comfortable with your CRM users having no restrictions on their access to ERP vendors.

> **Restrict the ability to export the vendor data**: Restrict access to the export data functionality to certain users, user roles, or user teams, such as the purchasing manager for example.

> **Restrict the ability to view and otherwise use the vendor data in CRM**: Restrict access to the vendor data to teams who directly use the data in day-to-day work, for example, the purchasing team.

# CRM UI changes

We will now identify the UI changes to CRM that will need to be made for the vendor management integration.

## Changes to CRM company screens

Vendor data will be synchronized to CRM and will be shown on the CRM company screens as a company of type "ERP vendor". Some of the data will be stored in new fields, which should already have been added to the UI for the contact management integration, meaning that no UI changes will be needed for our worked example.

**Make a note**

If your implementation is synchronizing different fields to the ones that we list in our worked example, you will need to make sure that they are displayed on the CRM UI.

A new UI rule will need to be added to ensure that vendors are read-only in CRM:

> When a CRM company is of type "ERP vendor", it should not be editable or deletable. This is because we are not synchronizing updates or deletes of customers from CRM to ERP.

If the company entity has a promote button to "promote" a CRM customer to ERP, you will need to make sure that the promote button is not visible for companies of type "ERP vendor", because we are not supporting the use case of promoting new vendors from CRM to ERP.

## UI changes to child entity screens

The child entities of a vendor are contact, address, phone number, and e-mail address. The screens which show the child entity data will now show the vendor child entity data as well.

A new UI rule will be added to ensure the vendor data is read-only:

➤ When contact, address, phone number, or e-mail address screens are showing vendor data, they should not be editable or deletable. This is because we are not synchronizing updates or deletes of contacts from CRM to ERP. It will be possible for an implementer to tell whether the data is vendor data because it will have the type "ERP vendor".

# Vendor integration with the CRM interactions feature

A key goal for the integration is to be able to use CRM interaction functionality with the new vendor data, to allow users to make phone calls, book appointments, send documents, and so on using the rich CRM functionality. As the vendor data will appear on the native CRM company screens, much of this workflow should be available without any additional development work.

There may be advanced interaction functionality that will still need to be configured, depending on the flexibility of your CRM application. Some areas to investigate are:

➤ **Document templates**: If your CRM allows for the creation, storage, and sending of pre-built document templates, you should consider whether there is documentation, such as RFPs, that is useful to vendors that you could create and add to CRM to improve the efficiency of the purchasing workflow.

➤ **Outbound call handling**: If your CRM provides outbound call handling functionality, you should consider whether there are useful outbound call handling scripts that can be added that will help with the management of your vendors.

➤ **E-mails**: If your CRM provides automatic e-mail, or e-mail template functionality, or other e-mail functionality, you should consider whether you can make use of it to improve your vendor management process.

➤ **Self service**: If your CRM provides a customer self-service portal, you should consider whether you wish to create a vendor self-service portal.

# Reports/dashboard changes

Now that we have brought the vendor records into CRM, we can make full use of the data by adding it to existing reports and/or dashboards, or new reports and/or dashboards. Some examples of new reports or dashboards that can be created are as follows:

➤ List of vendors in ERP that are currently inactive or active

➤ List of vendors in ERP that are currently on credit hold

➤ List of vendors sorted by credit limit

You should consider which vendor reports and dashboards would be beneficial for your business.

In the advanced workshop section, we discuss bringing vendor document transactions, such as purchase orders, to CRM, which will allow for more informative reports to be generated.

---

**Tip**

**Workshop**

- Gather together all the design work that you have completed for this chapter so far, and use the information to compile a list of UI changes that will need to be made.
- Decide which security restrictions you should impose for the newly synchronized vendor data.
- Define which reports and/or dashboards should be updated or created to make use of the new data which is available in CRM.

---

# Advanced workshop checklist

Now that we have designed a basic vendor management integration to improve the way your purchasing team manage their vendor accounts, we will consider some alternative features for the integration. This will allow you to tailor the functionality to make it more suitable for your business.

Evaluate whether you should make ERP vendor document transactions such as purchase orders, debit notes, credit notes, interest, prepayments, and payments available in CRM.

Synchronizing vendor data to CRM is very useful to the purchasing team, but if the vendor has questions about purchase orders, or about any document transaction history, the CRM user will still need to open up the ERP application to find the information. There are several strategies that can be considered, including synchronization, real-time views, screen pops, or a combination of the three:

> **Synchronizing vendor document transactions**: Vendor document transactions could be synchronized one way from ERP to CRM. The synchronization software could be updated to synchronize the data into new tables in the CRM database, and the CRM UI could be updated to show the data. This is similar to the use case for collections management integration, where invoices are synchronized to CRM for ERP customers. The benefit of synchronizing the data into the CRM database over other methods is that once the data is in the CRM database, it can be used more easily in CRM reports and dashboards. For example, if you synchronize purchase orders to CRM, you will be able to create reports on purchase order metrics, for example, ranking vendors on size of purchases ordered over time.

➤ **Real-time viewing of vendor document transactions**: Instead of copying the vendor transaction data into the CRM database, the information could be obtained in real-time views from the ERP API. This reduces the amount of data that needs to be copied to CRM.

➤ **Screen pop of vendor transactions screen**: A button or other launching mechanism could be added to the CRM UI to launch a screen pop of an ERP screen which shows vendor transaction data. The CRM user could launch this screen whenever they need to do a more detailed investigation of the document history of a vendor.

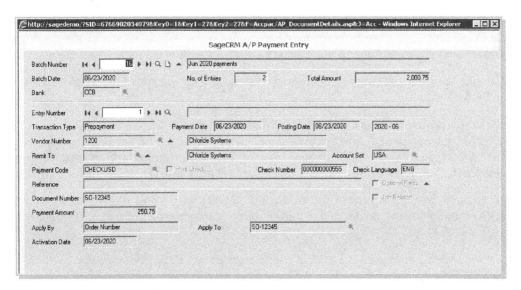

Evaluate whether you should implement a bulk import of vendors feature instead of, or as well as, synchronization of vendors.

This feature is similar to the bulk import feature for customers, which is discussed in some detail in the contact management chapter.

The bulk import of vendors feature will manually trigger a bulk import of all vendors from ERP to CRM. The feature can be kicked off with the user clicking a button in the integration administration area in CRM. The synchronization software, or other software, reads every vendor in the ERP database and copies it, in turn, to the CRM database. If the vendor record already exists in CRM, the vendor record in CRM is refreshed with the up to date ERP vendor record. If the vendor does not exist in CRM, a new vendor record is created to correspond with the ERP vendor.

The bulk import also needs to take into account vendors that have been deleted in ERP by detecting which ERP vendors have been deleted in ERP since the last bulk import and deleting them in CRM.

The bulk import of vendors feature has two immediate uses:

> ➤ When the vendor management integration is first deployed, all the vendor data will be in ERP, and none of it will be in CRM. This feature will copy all the vendor data to CRM, so that ERP and CRM will have the same list of vendors.

> ➤ The bulk import feature can be run occasionally, as a useful way to ensure that the vendor data is the same in both ERP and CRM.

For the vendor management integration, there is a third potential benefit of having a bulk import feature, which is that it can be considered as an alternative to a synchronization solution. If the vendor data in ERP does not change very often, then it may not be necessary to have a continuous synchronization solution, where changes to vendor data are detected and copied to CRM in real time, or near real time. In this case, evaluate whether you should only implement a bulk import that is run say once a week, rather than a synchronization solution. If you are time restricted, it is also useful to consider implementing a bulk import of vendor data as a first phase in a solution and bringing in continuous synchronization in a later phase.

Consider allowing CRM contacts, and other information, to be added to a vendor record in CRM.

CRM companies can have CRM-specific data associated with them, and in general, a CRM company can have many contacts associated with it. In our worked example, the vendors are read-only in CRM and only have ERP data with just one contact. This restriction is enforced by the integration developer in the CRM UI.

It is possible to allow editing of the vendor in CRM so that it is possible to add more CRM-only data to the vendor and to add contacts. Some examples of how this would be useful would be:

> ➤ Adding more data: In a CRM company, there can be lots of company information stored to help with customer management, such as:
>
>> ➤ Number of employees
>>
>> ➤ Company sector (industry sector)
>>
>> ➤ Company territory (geographical territory)
>>
>> ➤ Account manager (CRM user)
>
> It may be useful to be able to set these fields for the vendors that are synchronized from ERP.

> ➤ Adding more contacts: In a CRM company, there can be many contacts stored for a company, including any person who may be contacted, such as:
>
> > ➢ Marketing manager
> > ➢ Sales manager
> > ➢ Purchasing contact
> > ➢ Shipping contact

In a vendor that is synchronized from ERP, there will be only one contact, but it may be useful to be able to add more contacts to the vendor record that are only stored in CRM.

This needs to be designed carefully to make sure that the synchronization of vendors from ERP to CRM is not broken. Here are the rules to follow:

> ➤ If you are allowing the editing of a vendor in CRM, you should restrict the fields that can be edited to the fields which are CRM-only fields. That is, any field that is synchronized from ERP should not be editable, and any field that is not synchronized can be editable.
>
> ➤ If you are allowing the addition of contacts, you need to enforce that the contact that is synchronized from ERP is not editable, and any other contact can be editable. Contacts that are synchronized from ERP will have the type "ERP vendor contact", and so the rule can be that contacts of type "ERP vendor contact" are read-only.

# Summary

In this chapter, we designed a vendor management integration to add simple **vendor relationship management** (**VRM**) to your CRM application. The vendor synchronization scenario is a simpler version of the contact management integration, and a large proportion of code, schema, and UI reuse is possible.

We started off by describing a real-world scenario for our fictional RideRight Bike Parts Company, which has a need to implement vendor relationship management for the purchasing department. We identified the uses cases and reframed them as CRM workflows that we needed to implement:

> ➤ Ability to view ERP vendors in CRM, including:
>
> > ➢ Ability to use CRM interactions feature for vendors
> > ➢ Ability to view vendor analysis information in CRM reports and dashboards

We then designed the integration solution using the real-world applications of SageCRM and Sage ERP 300 to provide some context. We followed the same design steps outlined in the previous chapters.

We discussed the security implications of the changes we are making. Finally, we summarized the UI customizations that will be required for the vendor relationship management integration.

In the advanced workshop section, we discussed additional features and alternative solutions that can be considered:

> ➤ Ability to view document transactions for vendors in CRM
> ➤ Ability to do a bulk import of vendors, as well as, or instead of, synchronization
> ➤ Ability to add CRM contacts and other information to ERP vendors in CRM

At this point, the design is completed for the vendor management integration. The next step is to develop the solution. The chapter How to Develop and Maintain an Integration talks about the next development stage in more detail.

In the next chapter, we design a **support management integration**. The support management integration is an integration feature to improve support team workflow by using ERP information in CRM.

# How to Build a Support
# Management Integration

In this chapter, we look at how to make an integration to improve the support management workflow. The support team has benefited indirectly from some of the previous integrations, and in particular they now have accurate, up-to-date customer lists. However, they may still benefit from an integration with ERP.

We will look at how to make the support workflow more efficient, improving the support ticket management workflow by linking CRM with the ERP features for return material authorizations (RMAs). As usual we will start by defining some real-world integration use cases for our fictional company RideRight Bike Parts Company.

## Support management integration use cases

The RideRight Bike Parts support team is a small team that handles customer complaints. Customer complaints include issues that can be handled by the CRM ticket management feature, such as questions related to the delivery of ordered goods, for example late deliveries, missing deliveries, and incomplete deliveries.

Customer issues can also include issues that cannot be handled by the CRM ticket management feature, such as returned goods. Goods may be returned because they are defective in some way, or because the customer has decided they do not want them any more. Customers who return goods may receive a credit note, or replacement goods, both of which need to be processed in ERP using the RMA feature.

In some scenarios, a company may repair a defective product and return it to the customer, but for our use case, RideRight does not repair defective goods. They may send returned items to the original vendor who may or may not perform a repair.

The support team does not like having to do some of their work in CRM and some of their work in ERP.

The use case that we need to use for the support team is that they would like to be able to use the CRM application for all their customer tickets including the ones that currently need to be processed in the ERP application. This will improve support team efficiency and allow for more complete reporting on customer support status from CRM.

# Integration workflows

The use cases that are required for the RideRight support team can be converted to new integration workflows, as follows.

The support team should have the ability to create RMAs from the CRM ticket management feature, as part of the ticket management workflow.

# How

A new button will be added to the ticket workflow that will launch a screen popup for the RMA feature in the ERP. The following diagram shows the support management integration workflow:

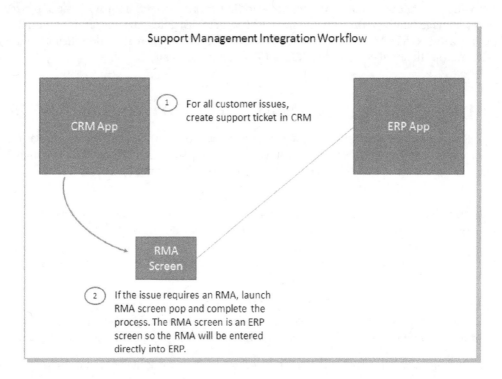

All support issues will be logged in CRM. When necessary, an RMA screen can be launched from CRM to enter an RMA.

The workflow for the support team will be what they will create a support ticket for every customer complaint that is raised. If the support user needs to create an RMA in ERP, they will launch the RMA screen from CRM in the context of the support ticket, and enter the RMA. The support ticket will be updated to show that an RMA was created.

This allows the CRM user to handle all types of support tickets from the CRM application. Reports and dashboards in CRM will be able to show whether the ticket was an RMA or a normal support ticket.

## Steps 1 to 5 – designing the workflow

The next step is to design the workflow. We shall use the real-world applications of SageCRM and Sage ERP 300, so that it is a realistic design.

In our worked example, we do not need to synchronize data so we do not need to do the first five steps of our design process; create entity diagrams, map the entity diagrams to each other, define the unique identifiers, define the fields and field mappings, or define the CRUD rules.

## Step 6 – designing the screen popups

We have skipped the first five steps of our design process as they are not needed for this workflow. The next step is to design the screen pops.

The button to launch the screen pop will be on a support ticket summary screen. Clicking on the button will launch the screen pop:

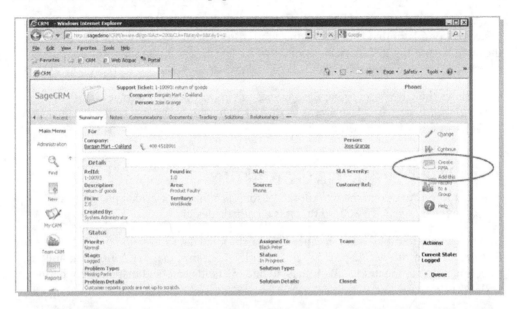

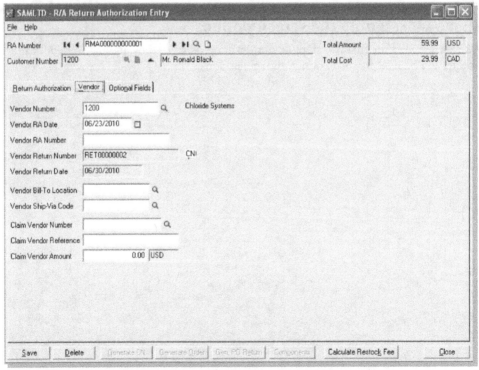

*Screenshot of the RMA screen in Sage 300*

The software to launch the screen popup should also update the support ticket and support ticket history with the information that an RMA has been created. This could be done by updating the description, problem type, or area, of the case details.

Once the RMA screen popup has been launched the user will be able to enter the RMA and save it in the ERP.

# Security

By default, any CRM user who has access to the support ticket area of CRM will be able to launch the RMA screen popup. Consider whether you should only make this button available to some CRM users, for example just the support team.

# CRM UI changes

The section on design of the screen popup covers the UI changes.

It is also useful to consider whether new reports or dashboards should be created to show information such as:

- How many support tickets result in RMAs being created
- Who are the top customers who return goods
- What are the top goods that are returned because they are defective

# Advanced workshop checklist

There are some additional steps that we can take to improve the richness of this support management integration feature:

- **Consider synchronizing the ERP RMA data so that it is viewable in CRM**: In our support integration we allow the user to create RMAs directly in the ERP. If the support user wishes to look at the RMA information later, they will need to use the ERP. Consider synchronizing the RMA data to CRM so that it can be viewed later from the CRM UI. There are two tactics to consider: one is synchronizing the RMA information to a new entity in CRM, and the second is to synchronize the RMA information into the support ticket database table so that it can be viewed as a type of support ticket. The first option is similar to the collections management integration, where invoices are synchronized one way from ERP to CRM. The steps to consider are:
  - Define the RMA entity and fields that are to be synchronized to CRM.
  - Create a mapping entity and fields in CRM to map the RMA data to. Include a customer reference and a unique reference.
  - Implement the synchronization.
  - Implement UI screens to show the RMA information.

The second option is similar to the vendor management integration, where we synchronize vendor data into the already existing customer entity in CRM. The steps to consider are:

> ➢ Define the RMA entity and fields that are to be synchronized to CRM.

> ➢ Map the RMA entity to the CRM support entity and the RMA fields to the CRM support fields. Create new fields if necessary. Include a customer reference and a unique reference.

> ➢ Define the type of a synchronized RMA record to be a predefined type, such as "RMA" so that they can be distinguished from normal CRM support tickets.

> ➢ Implement the synchronization.

> ➢ The RMAs will appear automatically in the CRM support ticket UI. Implement a UI change to make sure that they are read-only in CRM.

> ➢ If synchronizing the RMAs back to CRM, consider linking them with invoices, if invoices are synchronized to CRM: RMAs in ERP can be linked with an invoice. If you decide to synchronize the RMAs to CRM, and if you are already synchronizing invoices to CRM for collections management, you can decide to link them in CRM. This will allow, for example, users who are viewing invoices in CRM to be able to click through to related RMAs, and vice versa, users who are viewing RMAs in CRM will be able to click through to the related invoice. The changes to do this will require synchronization changes, and changes to the UI, to allow the link between invoices and RMAs.

> ➢ **Consider linking RMAs to vendors, for vendor returns**: It is possible to create a type of RMA called a vendor return, where returned goods are returned to the originating vendor. If you are synchronizing vendors to CRM and you are synchronizing RMAs to CRM you could link the two records together. This would allow a user who is viewing a vendor in CRM to click through to the related RMAs, or a user who is viewing vendor returns could click through to the related vendor.

# Summary

In this chapter, we described a real-world scenario for our fictional RideRight Bike Parts company, which needs to improve the support management workflow by linking it with the ERP RMA feature.

We identified the use cases and reframed them as CRM workflows that we needed to implement. The support team should have the ability to create RMAs from the CRM ticket management feature, as part of the ticket management workflow.

We then designed the integration solution using the real-world applications of SageCRM and Sage ERP 300, to provide some context. As this integration only uses screen popups we could skip most of the usual design steps and just talk about the location of the screen popup mechanism.

In the advanced workshop section, we discussed ways to improve the feature:

- ➤ Synchronizing the ERP RMA data so that it is viewable in CRM
- ➤ Linking synchronized ERP RMA data to invoices in CRM
- ➤ Linking synchronized ERP RMA data to vendors in CRM

At this point the design is completed for the support management integration. The next step is to develop the solution. *Chapter 8, How to Develop and Maintain Your Integration*, talks about the development stage in more detail.

# >8

# How to Develop and Maintain Your Integration

Up to this point in the book we have focused on integration architecture and design. If you have followed along with us, you may have already chosen which integration features are the most beneficial for your CRM and ERP applications, and which integration architecture and design you are going to follow. If you have completed the workshops you will have a very detailed design of what you are going to implement that is suited for your CRM and ERP application.

This chapter discusses the tasks that a project manager for the integration will need to consider when developing and maintaining the integration. We will cover the following areas:

> ➤ Development phase: Once the design is complete, the software needs to be written. We will talk about some strategies for project managing a simple software integration project.

> ➤ Deployment phase: We talk about the deployment of the integration feature starting from development completion, to having a live system with real users using the new integration features. We discuss tasks that need to be managed such as training, deployment plan, and managing user feedback.

> ➤ Ongoing maintenance phase: We talk about planning the long-term maintenance of the integration features, such as upgrades, enhancements, defect resolution, and other tasks.

## Development plan

A project manager will manage the development of the integration. The role of the project manager is to ensure that there is management buy-in for the project, and that all the features get built to an appropriate level of quality, and within an acceptable cost and timeframe.

We are going to discuss the development plan using an example one of the integration features that we have already designed, the contact management integration.

Instead of using a formal project management methodology, we will define a process that is as lightweight and flexible as possible. Feel free to use any alternative methodology that you prefer. We shall organize the development effort by work area. For each work area we shall create a list of user stories to be implemented.

# Work areas

Breaking the work into areas allows more than one person to work on the feature at the same time. The following diagram shows three work areas that the development work naturally falls under, and the optional installation work area:

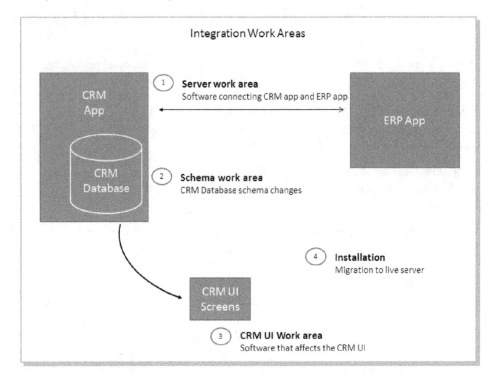

Integration development work can be broken down between server work, and UI work, linked by database schema work, in the middle:

> **Server work**: Server work is any software that runs on the CRM server, or the ERP server and is involved in connecting the CRM application with the ERP application. It includes all the synchronization software, such as the synchronization engine, and plugins, and it may also include server code that is needed for the real-time views and the screen popups.

> **Schema work**: The schema is the common point between much of the server work and the UI work. It includes any new tables or changes to existing tables that need to be made. Generally, the schema changes should be agreed first and then the server work and UI work can proceed independently once it is complete.

> ➤ **UI work**: UI work is any software that runs on the UI or connects the UI to the CRM server. It includes new screens, lists, reports, dashboards, buttons for launching screen pops, and any UI rules that need to be written, such as making records read-only, and any UI based security restrictions.

> ➤ **Installation**: If the integration feature needs to be migrated to the live CRM and ERP servers, installation work may need to be carried out.

# User stories

Within each work area, we shall break the work into small manageable chunks that we will call user stories, after the concept of user stories in the Agile software development methodology. A user story, for our purposes, is the description of a small feature that can be delivered by a developer and tested by a tester in one complete piece. It is recommended to keep user stories as small as possible.

The stories can be simply recorded in a spreadsheet, or a more specific user story tracking application can be used if you would like. The user stories should be listed in the order that they need to be delivered. Then the stories are developed, and tested one by one. Here is an example of user stories listed:

| Schema Stories | Estimate (days) | Start Date | End Date | Status |
|---|---|---|---|---|
| 1) Implement customer schema changes, adding new customer fields. | 1 | 5-Jun | 6-Jun | Complete |
| 2) Implement contact schema changes, if any. | 0.5 | 6-Jun | 6-Jun | Complete |
| 3) Implement address table changes, if any. | 0.5 | 6-Jun | 6-Jun | Complete |
| 4) Implement phone table changes, if any. | 0.5 | 7-Jun | 7-Jun | In Progress |
| 5) Implement email address table changes, if any. | 0.5 | 7-Jun | 7-Jun | Not Started |
| ..... | | | | Not Started |
| ..... | | | | |

In the following sections, we shall take a look at the first few user stories for each of our work areas for the contact management integration.

# Schema work area story examples

Based on the work needed for the contact management integration, the first five stories for the schema work area could look something like this:

> ➤ Implement customer schema changes, adding new customer fields

> ➤ Implement contact schema changes, if any

> ➤ Implement address table changes, if any

> ➤ Implement phone table changes, if any

> ➤ Implement e-mail address table changes, if any

# Server work are story examples

The first four stories for the server work area could look something like this:

1. **Synchronization of create customers from ERP to CRM**: Implement the synchronization of one customer record from ERP to CRM (where the customer does not exist in CRM, so that it is a create of a customer in CRM). Make sure all fields are mapped correctly, and the unique identifiers and types are set correctly.

2. **Synchronization of customer updates ERP to CRM**: Implement the synchronization of one customer record from ERP to CRM (where the customer does exist in CRM, so that it is an update of a customer in CRM).

3. **Bulk synchronization ERP to CRM**: Implement the synchronization of multiple customers from ERP to CRM (where some of the customers already exist and some of the customers do not already exist in CRM).

4. **Synchronization promote CRM to ERP**: Implement the synchronization of a newly promoted CRM customer to ERP.

---

**Make a note**

The server work is the largest work area. The preceding stories shown can be broken down into more granular stories, in a real-world situation. Also, preparatory work is needed such as building a synchronization engine, and plugins that can be used as a framework for the features. This is nontrivial work, but as the work is different for each architecture, CRM, and ERP application I have not created sample stories for them here.

---

# UI work area story examples

The first three stories for the UI work area could look something like this:

1. **Changes for customer UI**: Add the new fields that will be shown on the customer screen.

2. **Customer UI**: Add any UI rules that are designed, such as, make ERP customer read-only.

3. **Customer UI**: Add the promote button for CRM customers that are to be promoted to ERP.

The other stories in the UI work area will cover changes for the remaining UI areas such as contact, address, phone, e-mail address, reports, dashboards, and security restrictions.

# Installation work area story examples

An installation is needed if the development of the integration features is done on a backup copy of the CRM and ERP, and the work needs to be migrated to the live server when it is complete:

1. Write a database schema script to install the schema changes on the live server.

2. If the synchronization engine is a Windows service decide how you will install the Windows service.

3. Itemize all the files that need to be manually copied to the live servers, or write a small install script to install all the files to the live servers. You may need to install files on both the CRM server and the ERP server.

4. Write an installer for all the CRM UI changes. This is dependent on which CRM you are using.

# Estimates

A project management task is to provide estimates for the scope of the project. This includes estimating how long the project will take to deliver and how many people need to be working on it.

A simple project plan built in a spreadsheet, showing start date, completion date, and who is working in which area is shown in the following figure:

| | 5-Jun | 12-Jun | 19-Jun | 26-Jun | 3-Jul | 10-Jul | 17-Jul | 24-Jul | 31-Jul |
|---|---|---|---|---|---|---|---|---|---|
| Server Work | John | John | John | John | John | John | John | John | John |
| | | | | | Jasper | Jasper | Jasper | Jasper | |
| Schema Work | Jasper | | | | | | | | |
| UI Work | | Jasper | Jasper | Jasper | | | | | |
| Installation | | | | | | | | | Jasper |

At the start of the project, estimates can be gathered for each story to give the full scope of the project. As the project progresses and several stories are completed, the estimate can be revised when a true knowledge of how long a story takes is known.

You should also allocate time for getting the different work areas to integrate together. For example, the server user stories, to synchronize customers, need to work in conjunction with UI user stories, to display and promote customers. This will take testing time, and it is quite possible that some glitches will be found that will require some developer defect fixing or rework.

# Implementing the user stories

The stories will be implemented by a software developer who should also do unit testing. The features will then need to be tested independently by somebody who is not the developer, to make sure that they are implemented correctly.

For UI work, a CRM user could play the role of the tester, or the person who is being the project manager could also do it. For server-side work, a developer or technical person will need to run the test because there will be nothing to see on the UI side. A test on the server side may involve checking whether correctly formatted data has been copied to the correct place in the schema table.

Once a user story has been implemented and tested it is regarded as complete. If the story has a dependency on work from another area it will then need to go through integration testing. Once all the stories are finished, and they have all gone through integration testing, the integration project is complete.

---

**Make a note**

**Workshop**

Create a project plan for your integration:

- Assign a project manager for your integration project. (This could be you!)
- Define the integration project team, assigning developer and testing roles. (The tester and/or developer may also be you!)
- Define the work areas for your integration, and assign a developer and tester to each work area. It could be the same developer for all work areas.
- Define the stories for your integration for each work area. Make sure that the developer(s) and tester(s) review and understand the user stories.
- Order and estimate the stories. You can revise the estimates later after several stories have been implemented.
- Plan out regular meetings for discussing project status. It is up to you how often you wish to get the status for your project team, but weekly, or biweekly is a good rule of thumb.

---

# Deployment

Once the feature is complete it is time to push it out to the users. This should be also treated as a mini project to be managed. A lot of investment has gone into the feature and it is important to roll it out correctly, and ensure that all users are successfully using the feature.

Tasks to consider for the deployment are:

- ➤ Installation of the new integration feature
- ➤ Bringing users live
- ➤ Ongoing evaluation

# Installing the new integration feature

If you have implemented the integration feature on a copy of the live system, it will need to be installed on the live system. The installation should be done outside of office hours, so that there is no user downtime.

After the installation has been completed there should be some light re-testing carried out to make sure that it working as designed.

At this point you could consider asking one user to use the system for real, and give feedback. This is a good way to discover any unintended glitches in the development. When picking a user, try to pick a user who is more skeptical of the new system, rather than an obvious supporter. When the user gives an okay, it will be more convincing for the rest of the team.

When you do user testing at this final stage, be forewarned that it is very possible that the user will find something that needs to be corrected, or changed, to get the feature to work optimally. It is better to find out now, rather than later on, when everyone else is brought on board.

# Bringing users live

Users need to be trained to start using the new integration features.

Tactics for doing this depend on the size of the teams. If the team is small enough, everyone can be trained at the same time by demonstrating the features to them, and then sitting with the users for a day or so, while they get used to the features.

If the team is large, or if there are several teams, it is possible to train groups of users in staggered phases.

Training can be done formally in a classroom setting with the trainer or project manager demonstrating the new integration feature, or by providing documentation. It can also be done more informally, at the work station where the user is brought through the feature a few times by another user, before starting to use it independently.

In the initial stages, especially for the first day or so, it is recommended to have somebody on site to answer questions. It is important get full buy-in from the users. Avoid the scenario where a user gets stuck, becomes frustrated, and stops using the feature.

After the integration feature is rolled out and everyone is using it, you should provide users with a process for raising questions, and reporting defects. This could be anything from something simple like asking them to e-mail you or a more formal process could be used.

**Make a note**

**Workshop**

■ Define a project plan for the installation of your new integration feature

■ Pick a user to system test the integration feature on a live system

■ Define a plan to train users and deploy the integration feature to all CRM users

■ Define a process to allow users to raise issues after the integration goes live

# Ongoing maintenance

Ongoing maintenance of the integration is needed to keep it running smoothly over time. Tasks include:

➤ Fixing defects

➤ Periodic upgrades of ERP and CRM

➤ Data management: backups and manual synchronization

➤ Adding new integration features

# Fixing defects

As they use the system, users may find defects. Defects need to be triaged so that you fix the important ones and keep a note of the less important ones. Grading the defects on a scale of 1-5, where 1 is a showstopper and 5 is a cosmetic issue, is a useful way to determine which defects need to be fixed and in which order.

# Periodic upgrades of ERP and CRM

Over time you will need to manage the upgrades of the ERP and CRM software. If the integration is designed well and the development APIs are well designed, the integration features should still work after an upgrade, in most circumstances. However, it is possible that some rework, or changes, may be necessary. Always re-test the integration features after an upgrade.

# Data management – backups and manual synchronization

The data that is synchronized between the two applications needs to be monitored to make sure that that it remains consistent. If you are synchronizing data to CRM tables, monitor the size of the tables, and the performance of reads and writes to the tables. You may need to add indexes to the tables, or do other tweaks, to improve performance after a high volume of data is synchronized.

Make regular backups of the CRM and ERP database tables. You should be doing this anyway as part of normal server maintenance.

In the design sections for the integration features we talked about a manual synchronization feature to kick off an occasional manual synchronization to make sure that the data is all up to date and correct. Schedule time to run occasional manual synchronizations.

# Adding new integration features

Along with finding defects, users are also good at suggesting new features.

Keep a note of the new features, and evaluate which are worth doing, and in which order they should be done. Schedule time to implement new features and roll them out when appropriate.

**Make a note**

**Workshop**

Define a maintenance plan for your integration to cover the next two to three years

# Summary

In this chapter, we talked about the practicalities of developing, deploying, and maintaining an integration.

We looked at the project from the point of view of a project manager, and discussed the techniques of creating a project team, dividing out the effort into work areas, creating user stories, estimating, developing, and testing.

We then talked about deployment of the completed integration feature, by installing the software on the live server, and then training up users in groups, and working with them until they are using the new feature independently.

Finally, we discussed ongoing maintenance of the integration to keep it running smoothly over time. We discussed defect resolution, the need to retest after every upgrade of CRM and ERP application software, data maintenance, backups and tuning, and planning for new integration feature development.

In the next and final chapter, we wrap up by speculating about future developments in CRM to ERP integrations.

# > 9

# Where Next for Integrations – the Cloud and Other Areas

Software is always changing and as we reach the end of the book we have the opportunity to speculate on what is coming next for CRM to ERP integrations.

We shall start by considering the future of our sample company RideRight Bike Parts Company.

## The future of RideRight Bike Parts Company

RideRight Bike Parts Company is very happy with the integration functionality that they have developed but they want to continue to improve. They are considering some radical changes in the future to provide an even better customer and user experience.

The CRM and ERP applications that RideRight are using are currently installed on the company premises. Both applications going to be made available as cloud services in the next few years, and the IT Manager is considering moving his CRM and ERP deployments to the cloud.

Nearly all of the RideRight sales and support team have personal smart phones, and/or tablets, of one brand or another. They are comfortable using mobile apps, and they would like to use mobile apps as part of their work experience.

RideRight customers are used to order goods from companies such as Amazon and eBay on the Internet. They would like to be able to order everything from RideRight on the Internet as well.

The future technology directions that the RideRight business needs to consider are:

> ➤ Moving CRM and ERP to the cloud
>
> ➤ Making mobile apps available to the CRM users
>
> ➤ Make customer self-service and mobile apps available to the RideRight customers

These are also the directions that many businesses are heading in.

# Moving CRM and ERP to the cloud

The general direction of software deployments is to the cloud and if your CRM and ERP applications are currently on premise it is likely that you have, or will have, the opportunity to move them to the cloud in the future.

Some of the benefits of moving the CRM and ERP applications to the cloud are:

> ➤ It removes the support and maintenance responsibilities from the in-house IT department
>
> ➤ The CRM and ERP applications will be available to users all the time, 24x7
>
> ➤ The CRM and ERP applications will be accessible from everywhere, both inside and outside the company firewall
>
> ➤ There are potential savings to be made on operating costs

One disadvantage for integration developers is that software that runs on the cloud is typically less open to customization than software that runs on the customer's premise. In our integration designs, we assumed a relatively high degree of flexibility, and control, over how the CRM application can be customized to build an integration. There may now be an Internet firewall between the CRM and ERP application that was not there when they were both running on the same intranet.

In general, cloud deployments force an integration developer to stick more rigidly to supported interfaces and toolkits and this may require simplifying the integration workflow in places. If you are considering a move to the cloud, review how it will affect the integration functionality.

# Making mobile apps available to CRM users

Mobile apps are becoming more and more common in all areas of life, including work. Users of software applications will expect, more and more, to have at least some or most functionality available on a mobile app. A plan for the future should include a mobile app component.

Some benefits of mobile apps are:

> ➤ Users can use them at any time no matter where they are, such as at home, at work, on a customer site, or in a coffee shop

> ➤ Well-designed mobile apps are simple and intuitive to use, requiring little training or documentation.

> ➤ Mobile apps are easy to install and upgrade

Some disadvantages of mobile apps are:

> ➤ Mobile apps favor simpler workflows, over more complex workflows. Integration workflows tend to be more complex. Not all integration workflows may be suitable for mobile apps. For example, a complex order entry screen may need to be redesigned as a simple order entry screen, which will only work for basic orders for a mobile app.

> ➤ A different mobile app is needed for each smartphone platform, iPhone, Android, or Windows mobile. Consider standardizing your team on one platform to reduce support and development costs.

The timing of the development of a mobile app will depend on when, and if, mobile app development tools become available for your CRM application.

# Customers running things themselves

An ever increasing range of items can be purchased on the Internet. We now expect even local businesses, and not just large providers such as Amazon and eBay, to provide a customer website or mobile app to make orders and payments on.

Some benefits of having customers managing their own affairs on the Web or with a mobile app are:

> ➤ They can log on to the website or the app and do business with you at any time, from any place

> ➤ A well-presented website acts as a store front for your business and is able to bring in new customers without any user interaction, at any time

> ➤ Sales resources can be diverted to finding new sales or other areas of the business as less time is spent managing existing customers

A customer website or mobile app will not remove the need for human interaction with customers. There will still be sales, support, and marketing teams managing customer relationships with their CRM application. Orders and payments that are taken on the Web will still need to end up in the ERP application.

The website will therefore need to integrate both with the CRM application and the ERP application in order to provide a seamless business workflow. This can be done by extending the existing CRM to ERP integration to integrate with a customer website and mobile app features. The practicalities of doing this will depend on the tools and APIs that are available.

# Summary of the chapter

As we conclude our exploration of CRM to ERP integrations, we have taken some time out to discuss briefly some of the directions that future integrations between CRM and ERP are going.

All software is moving towards the cloud, and it follows naturally that we will need to produce integrations between CRM and ERP that work on the cloud, if you have not done so already.

Smart phones and tablets have already become a daily part of our lives for many of us. It is, again to be expected, that the integration features that we talked about in this book will become available in a user-friendly and possibly more simple form in a mobile app.

Our customers are becoming more and more familiar with managing their accounts on the Web and on mobile apps, and this again is something that will need to be provided to give a best class customer service.

# Conclusion

This book has been about how to build an integration between a CRM and an ERP application, from concept to delivery.

We have talked about the business benefits of an integration. We have discussed the different types of integration architectures that may be applicable for your organization. We talked about useful technologies such as synchronization options, real-time views, and screen pops, and the pros and cons of each technique.

We have designed, in great detail, several integration features that will benefit many areas of your customer-facing business.

We started with contact management as a basis for the other integrations. As we discussed contact management we also introduced you to the design methodology concepts such as user stories, workflows, entity diagrams and mappings, field mappings, and security considerations. We used these concepts again and again for each integration design.

After the contact management integration, we looked at other related integration designs. The sales management integration linked ERP sales orders and quotes with the CRM application. The collections management integration linked ERP overdue invoices with the CRM application. We then went on to talk about vendor management integration to provide a simple vendor relationship management tool within the CRM application, and we designed a support management integration to allow support users to manage RMAs from within CRM.

Each integration design included design workshops, so that you could design in parallel for your own applications. We gave ideas for reports and dashboards for each integration feature. We discussed security implications for all the new integrated functionality, and we discussed how management could make use of the new integrated information in CRM. In the advanced workshop sections in each chapter we discussed many simplifications, enhancements, and alternatives that could be considered as part of the design.

We talked about simple project management techniques for integration development, deployment, and ongoing support and maintenance. Finally, we spent a short amount of time on the future directions of CRM to ERP integrations.

By now, you have all most of the useful information that we can provide about building an integration between CRM and ERP.

All that remains is to wish you a fruitful and productive journey as you build your integration, and bring increased efficiencies and a more productive working environment to your team.

www.ingramcontent.com/pod-product-compliance
Lightning Source LLC
LaVergne TN
LVHW081343050326
832903LV00024B/1285